MW00945254

# Weak Bones, Strong Wills

The Stories of XLH

The XLH Network, Inc.

**The XLH Network, Inc.**
**911 Central Avenue #161**
**Albany, NY 12206**
**www.XLHNetwork.org**

The XLH Network, Inc., is grateful for the contributions of the patients and family members who shared their experiences here and for the volunteers in the patient-support community who came before us in creating the Network's original listserv and then creating and growing the more formal organization.

The XLH Network, Inc., is also grateful for the creativity of our cover artist, Danielle Sypher-Haley.

"What You Mourn" is reprinted with permission from CW Books.

Neither the publisher nor the writers of the essays contained in this book are medical professionals, and the information shared here cannot substitute for qualified, individual medical advice, or consultation. Please read our full disclaimer below.

**Weak Bones, Strong Wills, The Stories of XLH -- 1st ed.**

# CONTENTS

# INTRODUCTION

X-Linked Hypophosphatemia (XLH) and the related autosomal and tumor-induced hypophosphatemias are metabolic bone disorders characterized by the wasting of phosphorus, leading to soft, poorly mineralized bones.

That sounds pretty simple, right?

Even when you add in the whole panoply of related symptoms, it does not sound so bad. Just looking at the objective, quantifiable symptoms, we've got the following (to varying degrees, depending on the severity of the individual patient's condition): low phosphorus levels in the blood, bowed legs, malformed joints, rickets, osteomalacia, rachitic rosary, short stature, spontaneous dental abscesses, osteoarthritis, enthesopathy throughout the body, nephrocalcinosis, Chiari malformations, tinnitus, hearing loss, bone spurs, pseudofractures, microfractures, and stress fractures.

The medical terms are all so clinical and detached. They are just words. Boxes to check off on a chart. Lab numbers that are flagged as "abnormal." White spots or clouds on X-rays. No big deal.

But if you stop and think about it, you might realize that the XLHers aren't thinking in terms of "low phosphorus in the blood." We're thinking, "I'm exhausted all the time."

We're not thinking, "I have osteomalacia" or "I have improper mineralization of my bones." We're thinking, "It feels like my bone is broken. Sometimes multiple bones. Every single day. And when one stops hurting, another one starts."

We're not thinking, "My bones are soft." We're thinking, "My bones have bent so badly that I can't walk on them." We're not thinking "My posterior longitudinal ligament has calcified." We're thinking, "I can't twist my spine enough to take care of my personal hygiene."

Our bones are soft, our lives are hard, but we are strong and resilient. We persevere, despite all the challenges. But if there's one thing that can slow us down, it's the lack of solid information about the real-life consequences of our rare medical condition. There's so much about living with XLH that isn't in the scientific literature, either because it's never been studied, or because it cannot be reduced to numbers and graphs.

That's why we're here to tell the real stories of XLH and the people affected by it. Not the medical jargon, not the numbers and charts, but the real-life experiences of patients and their families.

# DIAGNOSIS

## The Science

Hypophosphatemia means "low phosphorus levels in the blood." In patients with XLH and the related phosphate-wasting disorders, it's caused by an excess of a hormone known as Fibroblast Growth Factor 23 (FGF23). The excessive production of the FGF23, in turn, is caused either by a genetic mutation (XLH and the autosomal hypophosphatemias) or by a tumor (Tumor-Induced Osteomalacia).

Phosphorus is required for strong bones (and teeth) and proper muscle function. Without a sufficient supply, patients may develop lower limb deformities (bow or knock-knees), short stature, spontaneous tooth abscesses in the absence of trauma or cavities, bone pain, muscle weakness and calcification of ligaments and tendons.

Since XLH and the autosomal hyposphosphatemias are genetic disorders, they can be transmitted to future generations. Tumor-Induced Osteomalacia is not well understood, but as its name suggests, it appears to be caused by a tumor, rather than a genetic defect.

In addition to inheriting XLH from a parent, it's possible for a spontaneous mutation of the gene to occur at conception, causing XLH to develop, and it is then heritable for future generations in that family.

Diagnosis is relatively straightforward when a parent has already been diagnosed with XLH, but there can still be challenges. Basic blood tests are not always reliable indicators. Sometimes, a parent with mild symptoms may not be aware that she has XLH, because she was a spontaneous case and never correctly diagnosed. In those cases, the parent gets the diagnosis as part of diagnosing the child! In one case, a father with XLH had a daughter who does not have XLH, which should be impossible according to the basic principles of transmission of an X-Linked dominant condition. He had the daughter's genetic test done twice, since the initial result ran contrary to what was known about genetic transmission. The test was correct, and initially he thought he might have had an autosomal version of hypophosphatemia. He wasn't genetically tested until much later, during a KRN23/burosumab trial, when it turned out that he did have the X-Linked dominant version of hypophosphatemia, but in a "mosaic" version, which is extremely rare.

Diagnosis is considerably more complicated when neither parent has XLH and the child's XLH is due to a spontaneous mutation. Genetic forms of hypophosphatemia are rare, affecting an estimated one in twenty-thousand births, so it's not something with which most pediatricians are familiar. The first obvious sign of a problem, bowed legs, can be discounted as an optical illusion from the child's diapers. Sometimes the wrong set of laboratory values is used for testing the blood phosphorus levels; normal pediatric phosphorus levels are higher than adult levels, so a child with a low pediatric level can still be higher than a low adult level.

Once it is clear that something is wrong with the child's bones, there are several blood tests, in addition to genetic testing, that may indicate XLH, including low phosphorus levels while calcium levels are normal; and elevated FGF23 levels.

The pattern of transmission for the more common X-Linked Hypophosphatemia is as follows:

**An XLH father** will: Always pass the affected gene to his daughters and never pass the affected gene to his sons.

**An XLH mother** will *with each pregnancy*: have a fifty percent chance of passing the affected gene to either sons or daughters.

For the autosomal variations, the pattern of transmission is described here: https://ghr.nlm.nih.gov/primer/inheritance/inheritancepatterns.

That's the science of diagnosis, but there's so much more to understand about going through the experience as a patient or family member.

## Mommy Memories
## by Joyce Olewski Inman

I often wonder how other parents of children with spontaneous cases of XLH discover that their child has XLH—what their thoughts and experiences were during those early (and long) days of diagnosis.

I will never forget looking at a friend of mine, a labor and delivery nurse, and telling her that we were going to take our daughter to see a doctor because her legs were still so bowed at the age of two. Nor will I forget her response: she told me she had thought I needed to do this for some time but didn't tell me because she was worried I would be offended. I will not forget the elderly woman in a McDonald's parking lot who told me I had nice legs, and then—when I expressed surprised thanks at her remark—pointedly asked me why I was not taking my daughter to the doctor to ensure that her legs were "fixed."

I will never forget crying in our pediatrician 's office when she told me she thought my daughter had nutritional rickets and that it was probably because I breastfed her and did not give her the recommended vitamin D drops. I won't forget the constant refrains of "don't worry" and "she will grow out of this" from pediatricians to orthopedists. And I will never forget the six months of "just one more test—there is no way this will come back positive, but let's check anyway."

I will never forget going to a cookie swap party at a friend's house the week we received our diagnosis and having to leave because I couldn't stop crying and was scared of our new unknowns.

This said, I also won't forget the moment two friends of ours who are emergency room physicians began sending us articles from medical journals and telling us it was going to be okay. I won't forget the long conversations with two founders of The XLH Network, Inc. and the encouragement and advice they gave me. I will never forget the first time I had a private email exchange with another mother whose child had XLH and sending one another pictures of our children who were both missing all of their front teeth from abscesses so they would both know there were other people like them.

I will always remember how this family from Canada called XLH "special bones" and how when she was really young this was a soothing way to talk to my daughter about why her legs hurt. I won't forget discovering via social media that this mother died unexpectedly and the grief I felt for a woman I had never met. I will never forget the day my daughter met another girl with XLH and the precious bond they developed—a bond they still have today, not one born of disease but simply born of friendship. Little girls being little girls.

I will never forget meeting our doctor and his research associate and the relief and confidence they gave me. I will not forget my daughter's strength and determination—her insistence on having control over her own body—and the day she told her doctor "I will walk for you, but I will not run for you." Her ability to compensate for her disability was amazing. Even as a preschooler she was spunky and strong.

Our goal as a family has always been to ensure that our daughter would get the best treatment possible and have the opportunity to try anything she wanted, and she has shown us over and over that this is a reality. She has been a dancer, a swimmer, and a softball player. Her latest love is gymnastics. She has the body of a gymnast, petite and strong. I do not know if her body will allow her to continue to do gymnastics, but I do know that if she wants to continue in this sport or any other that she will. She is an amazing child (I do realize I am quite prejudiced as I write this), and I am confident that she will touch the lives of others through her spirit and determination in the same ways that so many of the friends we have met through our XLH community have touched ours. We have visited the beaches of Rhode Island, explored New York City, learned to knit, eaten our first lobster, and begun the process of advocating for others—all because of a community that has embraced our daughter and helped us find our way.

# My Journey with XLH
# and the Lessons I Carry in My Bones
# by Sarah Quereau

My first memory of being an XLHer was in my doctor's office. I was very small, and my doctor had retired. His replacement was lovely, and she followed up with the excellent care that I had received. However, she was not MY doctor, and I wanted my doctor. I remember yelling his name in the waiting room and my new doctor coming out to reassure me. I adored both of my doctors, but did not know how truly fortunate I was to be in their care. At a time when little was known about XLH, I had, somehow, landed with doctors that knew how to treat it. Mine was a spontaneous case—the first in my family. But somehow, thankfully, my parents happened to make an appointment with someone who would learn all he could about it.

I have what is considered a mild case. Aside from bowed legs as a baby, which straightened with treatment, slight in-toeing, and a tooth abscess, I was pretty much asymptomatic as a child and young adult. I remember blood tests, followed by special lunches with my parents. I remember feeling special because I got to visit the school nurse every day to gulp down my bitter laxative-laced apple juice. As an adult, I have some mild symptoms—some joint stiffness and foot sensitivity, a few aches and pains. But the biggest part of my XLH journey has been that of a parent.

When my older daughter was born, my entire perspective of XLH changed (among all of the other life-
changing things about becoming a parent). From the
day of her birth (really before her birth) we began telling doctors that we were concerned. "I had rickets, and
not the nutritional kind," I told the OB-GYN, a genetic
counselor, the on-call hospital pediatrician, my daughter's pediatrician. That was the only name I was ever
given for it, rickets. I did not know, at that time, to call
it X-Linked Hypophosphatemia.

Looking back, I wonder if they would have listened
sooner had I referred to it as "X-linked," and therefore
an undeniably genetic condition. At every single pediatric appointment, I would remind the pediatrician of
my history. "Should we have some testing done now?"
I would ask. *Every. Single. Time.* "No, she is fine, I
don't think we need to worry about that," the pediatrician said. The pediatrician would reassure me through
my daughter's hip that "clicked" at birth, her almost unbearable sleep difficulties, and through the beginning
of tiny bowed legs. I watch videos of my daughter as a
toddler, and I am saddened. Her tiny, very obviously
bowed legs caused her to have to swing her legs out
from the hip to walk. The effort it would take her tiny
little body to run fills me with guilt. Why didn't I push
harder? Why didn't I insist or get a new doctor?

By the time the doctor finally listened to us, we had
been saying the same thing for sixteen months. We
were then referred to a pompous orthopedic surgeon.

Why that was the first referral, I still don't understand. So, after examining our tiny daughter, who had very obvious signs of what I now know to call XLH, the orthopedic surgeon stood in the hallway, leaned on a wall with his arms crossed and declared loudly and with jubilance (as if he had made a brilliant discovery), "Her mother had rickets. And SHE HAS rickets!!" Over and over he exclaimed this. He seemed so outwardly pleased with himself, telling us what we had been telling our doctor for the entirety of our daughter's life. He laughed a self-congratulating laugh and promptly referred us to a doctor two hours away that specialized in diabetes.

We didn't know that the doctor specialized in diabetes until we walked into the waiting room and were perplexed to see all kinds of information about blood sugar and foot health plastered on the walls. We were incredibly nervous, but we came to this appointment fully prepared. We'd done a LOT of research, we called XLH by its proper name, and came with a long list of questions. Finally armed with a diagnosis, we were not messing around. This poor doctor may not have known what hit her. She was kind, and to her credit, more than willing to admit that our child was beyond her area of expertise, but she was not expecting US. We fired question after question at her, and she stumbled to answer them. Several times, she opened her laptop to email a question to this other doctor that she knew of, who happened to be one of the leading experts on XLH.

The third time she did this, we stopped her, thanked her for trying to help, and asked how we could get an appointment with this other doctor.

A short time after that, we had our first appointment with him. As we walked into the building, I felt nervous anticipation. Would they really be able to help us? What would they say? How severe was her XLH? Would she need surgeries? Would she be permanently deformed? Would other kids make fun of her? Would this doctor be able to see us as regular patients? Would he actually listen to us? We had asked my mother-in-law to come along to help with our daughter so that we could just focus on talking with the doctor. The instant the doctor and his assistant walked into the exam room, I felt immense relief. They greeted us like family and made us feel immediately at home. They listened. They were sorry for our journey and that we hadn't been listened to. They were glad that we had ended up with them. We met an entire team of people that would help our daughter that day—the doctor, his nurse, the research assistant, physical therapist, and orthopedic surgeon, all of whom would follow her care as she grew.

And so our questions were answered and our worries eased. Our daughter would be okay. We knew that she was in the best possible hands. A great weight was lifted that day. We still had worries about her, but all of the sudden, we knew that we were doing exactly what she needed.

The decision to have a second child was complex for us. This time, we had the facts. We knew that each of my children would have a fifty percent chance of inheriting the gene mutation that causes XLH. We also knew that boys tend to be more severely affected than girls. I was very relieved when we found out we were having a girl. Not only because our older daughter would have a sister, but also because if she did have XLH it was more likely that her case would be milder, like mine and our older daughter's.

We worked with the specialist and had labs done with our younger daughter when she was just a tiny baby. Even though within a few months of her birth we knew that she didn't carry the gene mutation, the wait was still agonizing. We were so relieved that she did not have XLH. As a parent, you hope that your child doesn't encounter things that might make their life more challenging. However, in the big picture, XLH is not the worst thing that could happen.

That experience made me realize that I did not want to go through that again. I did not want to have any more biological children, partly because of XLH, and partly for other reasons. If we grew our family further, it would be through adoption. This decision is so complex and personal. I would never fault another XLHer for deciding otherwise. Our daughters are both incredible human beings, and our lives are truly richer because of them. But we all have to weigh both ends and decide what is best for us—for our own families.

It is something nobody told me when I was a kid with "rickets," that one day I would have to decide whether to risk passing my condition on to my child. And that they could have a more severe case than mine. Nobody prepared me for the weight of that.

As I get older, I do notice more aches and pains. I have a calcium deposit on my foot that makes it difficult to wear certain shoes. I recently began taking calcitriol (after having not taken medicine for XLH in twenty-five years or so) and noticed that I was less achy. My ankles were no longer stiff in the morning, I had more energy. I hadn't even realized that XLH was taking a toll on my body until I began the medication and started feeling better. I try to stay active—Zumba and yoga are my favorites right now. I do worry about what will happen with my body as I age, but so far, I am able to do all of the things that I want to do.

I have learned so many important things from having XLH—life lessons that will be with me forever, lessons that I carry in my bones. From my journey with XLH, I have learned empathy. Humans have so many beautiful differences that need to be celebrated. I have learned to practice self-compassion. There are times when I can push myself and times when I need to listen to my body. It is important to take care of myself. I have learned that what you see as a weakness may one day become an asset.

I have learned the importance of community—our doctors, team of specialists, and other parents. Through one of my daughter's specialists, I met other parents of kids with XLH. I value these friendships immensely. One parent in particular has been a rock for me (whether she knows it or not), and is a beautiful reminder of bravery and strength. Her daughter's friendship with my daughter is so important to her and to us. She has a friend who "gets it." A friend who is special and different in some of the same ways that she is. And, even though they see one another infrequently, they pick up right where they left off every time.

I have learned to go with my gut and not to be afraid to question doctors or to disagree with them, to demand better care, to demand answers, and to walk away and find someone else if necessary. My health, and my children's health are worth fighting for. I have learned to be grateful for each moment. None of us know what our future looks like. I have learned to be grateful for my body—with all of its "imperfections." My body is pretty amazing, and I am thankful for the things my body allows me to do. I have learned how to parent a child who has the spunk and the strong will to push past her challenges and to be the very best that she can be. I have learned to trust my child's determination—to step back and let her discover how far she can push herself. I have learned that my child has more determination and strength than many other children her age, and I have learned that she will be okay, that we will be okay.

I have learned that we are all okay, in our own strong and beautiful ways. I know this in my bones.

# EARLY YEARS

## The Science

At present, there is no official "standard of care" for XLH children (or adults). Generally, though, pediatric patients are seen by pediatric endocrinologists (specialists dealing with the endocrine system and hormones), their blood is tested for levels of phosphorus (among other things), and they may be x-rayed for evidence of rickets (soft/weak bones in children, prior to closing of growth plates).

Specific treatment methods may vary depending on the severity and complications of each individual case. At present, treatment requires a delicate balance of activated vitamin D (calcitriol) and oral phosphate (such as K-Phos or Neutra-Phos). Treatment must be monitored by a clinician to minimize the potential consequences of treatment, including secondary hyperparathyroidism, hypercalcemia and nephrocalcinosis.

In some cases, the pharmacological treatment is sufficient to strengthen and straighten the leg bones, but in other cases, orthopedic surgery may be recommended.

For more information, the journal article, "A Clinician's Guide to X-Linked Hypophosphatemia," is a good start. You can read it here: https://www.ncbi.nlm.nih.gov/pmc/articles/PMC3157040/.

In addition, XLH children may experience a variety of dental issues in their baby teeth, adult teeth or both. They include spontaneous abscesses in the absence of trauma or cavities and delayed eruption.

## Horse Pills and Little Footballs

Some young XLHers had surgery, some didn't; some wore braces, some didn't; some were teased, some weren't. But the one thing they almost all had in common was having to take disgusting-tasting medicine and hating it.

The powdered and liquid forms were particularly noxious-tasting, and a common anecdote involves toddlers not just learning to swallow pills at an incredibly early age, but insisting on it, so as to avoid the other versions. One parent reports that initially she hid the calcitriol inside a sultana (raisin), and her infant son would then eat the sultana. "Until one day, I noticed that he pulled the capsule out of the sultana, threw the sultana over the edge of the high chair and swallowed the tablet without any water or liquid. He never looked back." On the other hand, if you have a child who is having trouble learning to swallow a pill, check out this video: http://research4kids.ucalgary.ca/pill-study.

Quite a few young XLHers found ingenious ways to avoid taking the stuff, but we'll spare the parents reading this from giving their kids any ideas for where to hide spit-out pills!

Another way that XLHers (and parents) found to cope with the horrible pills was to give them nicknames. One patient reported calling the pills Tic Tacs. (Although, trust us, they don't taste anything like candy!) The dissolvable Phosphate Sandoz tablets got the nickname of "bomb drinks" from their effervescence.

Sometimes the names referred to the shape of the pill. One person recalled referring to the phosphorus supplement as "the big white one" (it really is a large pill, the sort that even adults might refer to as "horse pills") and the gel-cap of activated vitamin D as "the little football."

One parent referred to the phosphorus powder as "growing medicine" to induce the reluctant child to take it before he switched to pills at age three. The calcitriol (activated vitamin D) was referred to as "squirty medicine."

Another parent calls the phosphorus the "crunch" pill and the activated vitamin D the "poppy" pill, encouraging the child to crunch the one and pop the other. She explained, "A trick I used when he was younger to get him to chew them properly is to make them crunch nd pop in an attempt to surprise Daddy, who also played along by reacting shocked or like it made him jump."

In the 1970s and earlier, the activated vitamin D was often prescribed as a liquid, rather than the more convenient gelcaps we have now. One XLHer recalls that he was prescribed "forty drops" twice a day, so it was referred to as "drops."

Some kids didn't take well to any of the parents' attempts to make the medicine palatable; one child called hers the "mean pills."

And finally, a German XLHer, Helmut Barz, had some unique experiences with medications:

*As a small child, I got my phosphate in liquid form, either referred to as Salzwasser (salt water), because it tasted very salty, my "Schnäppschen" (my little schnapps) because I drank it from a tiny glass usually used for schnapps, or my "Zaubertrank" (magic potion) referring to the Asterix comic books.*

*My Vitamin D (no calcitriol in my youth) was usually called by its brand name "Vigantol." After reading "Pippi Longstocking," my mum and I also started to call it my "Krumulus pill," which is a magic pill Pippi gives her friends for NOT growing up. We changed the magic spell accordingly, asking the pill to make me big and strong.*

*These days I love to refer to my medication as "Meine Drogen." "Drogen" = "drugs," once a legitimate German word for medication but nowadays usually referring to illegal drugs.*

*A while back, my alarm for taking my next round of pills went off while I was walking home through a crowded street. As I usually have my medication on me, I took them out of my backpack and just as I was about to swallow my pills, I got stopped by a police officer demanding to know what I was taking. So I explained to him that this was basically just minerals and vitamins (Phosphate, Magnesium and Calcitriol—okay, I was stretching the definition of vitamin a bit). He didn't believe me. Lucky for me, my doctor had his practice nearby so the police officer walked me there. My doctor gave him a piece of his mind.*

# The Braces
# by Chris Younger

The day was rather typical; I was going to my parents' house to help clean out the attic. The accumulation of stuff showed the evidence of nine kids and a bunch of grandkids. Boxes of old toys, baby items, school projects—you name it, it was there. I was going through a box and out of the corner of my eye I saw something. It was one of those double- and triple-take moments where I knew what I was seeing, but at the same time also couldn't believe it. At the same time I was having flashbacks to some of my worst childhood memories. They were leaning against the wall, and as if talking to me—no, more like taunting me—there was an air of arrogance, a superiority, a smugness in the way they leaned against the wall. Yes, it was my childhood nemesis, the one thing I hated the most, the ever-dreaded "braces."

The braces—I had many other names for them, and I don't know if there was an official name for them other than braces—were circa 1965 or about, though the dates get a little fuzzy. I believe I was around four years old when they appeared in my life. For those not familiar with this contraption let me try to describe. Think of a cross between the ugliest baby shoes imaginable and a Frankenstein boot. On each side of the shoe there is a metal bar attached that ran straight to the hip on the outside, with the inner bar running to the middle of the thigh's cross-strap. The outer bars were attached to an oval metal bar that went around the waist. There were leather straps at the waist, the thigh and the shin. The shoes and hips were hinged but there was no bending of the knees. Yes, these could be in a torture museum. Walking, if you can call it that, was straight legged. Think of old horror flick zombies or the North Korean military.

Getting into the braces was rather eventful. Take a curved leg and try to fit it inside two straight pieces of metal, like this diagram: |(| |)|. Now in my case my legs were bowed wider than the metal spacing, so my legs had to be jammed into the space. I guess this was the therapeutic part. I don't know if the braces were to prevent further bowing or to help straighten my legs, with the thought that under constriction the bones would magically grow straight. In any event, most of the day was spent in the braces.

I developed several techniques of avoidance when it became braces time. First, scream bloody murder. Most times I was forcibly put into the things. Mom would yell out to the neighbors, "Yes, he's ok, just braces time." Second, hide. I couldn't be put in the braces if they couldn't find me, so I found some of the best hiding places in and out of the house. Once all my hiding places were discovered I came up with the third trick: hide the braces. "Nope, never saw them. Braces? What braces? Never saw them, don't know where they got to." Finally, fourth, remove the braces and lie low, out of the radar. With nine kids this was easier than you would imagine.

I do feel sorry for my parents because I put them through a living hell with these things. As a high-energy four-year-old, I could do everything that everyone else was doing and keep up with my siblings, except when I was wearing the braces. My older brother reminded me of the game they used to play throwing magnets at me, and if they stuck to the metal it was worth a point. Such a loving family.

The braces were short-lived, but were definitely a PTSD-inducing experience. I don't recall how long I had to wear them actually, and don't know if it was due to me being so difficult or whether the doctors came up with the next therapy, daily mega doses of vitamin D, but that's another story....

*Editors' note: You can see a picture of Chris's braces here:* www.xlhnetwork.org/weak-bones-strong-wills. *Another type of braces was also in common use in the 1900s. It's called a "foot abduction brace" or "boots and bar orthotic," and consists of two shoes affixed to a bar that runs between them. It's seldom used today for XLH patients, but has uses for other conditions. For more information and a diagram, see* https://www.ncbi.nlm.nih.gov/pmc/articles/PMC2958265/.

# The Pink Liquid
# by Kimberly Murray

From as far back as my memory bank will allow, I remember drinking this nasty, pinkish color liquid ALL DAY LONG. So maybe not literally all day long, but five times a day sure felt like it. I would fight my mother with every inch of my physical force and my vocal power. "I hate it! I don't care what happens if I don't take it! It's nasty! Please don't make me drink it, Mommy!" Those are just a few of the tantrums I used to throw.

I remember calling every hospital and medical center in my area and asking them to please create a pill for me to take instead of the powder mixture I was taking five times a day. They thought I was being a funny, silly, little girl. At eight years old, my resources were limited. If the internet was even around then, it sure wasn't in my household. All I had was a phone book, and I figured that was a good place to start. The few times someone actually listened when I called, they knew nothing of this rare disease. They couldn't even pronounce it. There I was, a third grader, able to spell it out, sound it out, and give a child's version of what it was exactly: "I have to wear braces on my legs because it makes me walk funny and I have to have an operation to fix me."

The age-old question every child is asked: What do you want to be when you grow up?

"I want to be a scientist so I can invent a pill for my medicine," was always my answer. Thankfully, a pill was made available before I committed to studying science and medicine. I sucked at chemistry.

Looking back now, I was just a young girl begging for someone to listen to me, to hear my needs as a person with a rare disease. No one knew what I was going through. Not even the team of doctors and nurses who were treating me. It was even worse in gym class at school. After trying and trying to keep up with my classmates and friends, I just couldn't run as fast, jump as high, or keep up with their amount of energy. I ended up needing a doctor's note stating I should be allowed to sit out when my legs were hurting. Well, that was all the darned time. I didn't want any of the other kids knowing this, so I probably pushed myself more than I should have, but that is just my personality. I don't like to quit. I don't like to be told I can't do something. I'm pretty sure this disease made me like this. Strong-willed, independent, and persistent.

# Clinical Trials
# by Sanders Inman

It all started when I tried out for the first clinical trial for the new treatment, KRN23/burosumab, but my kidneys had too much phosphate, so I could not get into the trial. I had to lower my medicine, only taking it three times a day instead of four times a day. Now that I'm in the trial I don't have to take any pills; instead I take shots. I like taking the shots better, but they hurt a little. But I am a star patient so nothing hurts me because I'm tough.

When I first started the trial I had to go every two weeks for four months. I missed a lot of school but thanks to my wonderful teacher, Mrs. Lisa, I didn't get behind. Once I finished going every two weeks, I went every month for five months, then I went every two months for five months. Today was my sixty-four-week visit which I considered my last visit, and we found out I only have to go every six months. That is a big change from going every two weeks. Most of all I'm so excited that I only have to go every six months. That is my story about my journey of KRN23/burosumab.

# Bionic Woman in Training
# by Latrell Castanon

I was adopted as a baby. My adoptive parents (I call them Momma and Daddy) didn't know what was in store for them, but it was a wild ride to say the least. God obviously had His hand in it, because I have the same color eyes as my Momma, I had the same birthmark mole on the back of my shoulder as her, and her whole family is oddly genetically very short. Huge blessings come in small packages? I believe this had a huge impact on me growing up, since I felt not so different from my family. Of course, I knew I was and I felt it in my bones for sure, but at least the stigma of being short in stature was lessened to a large extent.

I remember going to the hospital a lot, after the initial diagnosis at age two with what they called Vitamin D Resistant Rickets (VDRR) (which I remember only vaguely; I remember going yearly to be exact). I remember the blood draws, though oddly enough, I don't remember them bothering me that badly, and I thought I was pretty brave. (Don't let me fool you though, it took an army to give me a shot in the derriere). I remember the wonderful nurses who worked at the hospital in Dallas (why I became a nurse), and most of all I remember Dr. Worthington, the doctor who I would see nearly every time I went. I believe he was a metabolic bone doctor, an endocrinologist, but he was great, and I actually looked forward to seeing him every year.

The greatest impact I remember from the disease when I was young was pain. My legs ached whenever I had to complete the mile walk for physical education in school. I am pretty sure that the physical education teacher thought I made it up, but I took longer than everyone else and tried. It wasn't what I wanted, because I remember wanting to be faster and stronger. I think this is when my fascination with super heroes started. I wanted to be the bionic woman so badly!

As my mother can attest, I never let it slow me down when I was little, but it did affect walking, running, and jumping. My mom put me in dance class and I remember being really good at gymnastics, but I could never jump as high as the other girls and it made me mad! Being in dance class ended up bringing another blessing. My dance teacher heard me singing some of the songs the older girls were dancing to, and was like, "You can sing?" She told my mom and that is what started my singing career. Though I never became famous, it has brought me blessings and was instrumental in building my self-esteem.

Slowly but surely, dancing and gymnastics became more difficult. They came to a complete halt when I started having severe pains in my neck and my left leg. All the orthopedic doctors could see was an osteochondral defect in my spine. Later in life this would be significant, but initially I just waited for the pain to pass, as I learned to do often throughout my life.

# Helpless? Not Me!
## by Carol from Missouri

*Stuck! I got as far as I could, but I found myself straddling the metal rail and looking down at the shiny hard floor miles below me. Not sure what to do! Not sure how to get down! But they are leaving without me! They forgot me! What do I do now?!?*

*Abandoned. Hope fades away. Despair and fear settle in. And I am still stuck!*

*Some strange lady in a white dress, funny hat, and squeaky shoes notices me and rushes over to my prison. Caught! The next thing I know I'm flat on my back looking up at a huge net over my bed. Trapped! No way out now! How will I ever get home? I am all alone.*

They say your first memory shapes the person you become. I think it did.

I was barely two years old when my parents had to leave me at Children's Hospital for the first time. It was the first of too many times, as the doctors tried to figure out why my bones were soft, why my legs were bowing, and why I was shorter than I should be. It was the beginning of a lifetime of blood tests, X-rays, and all sorts of other procedures. But never again did I let myself get caught. My sisters will tell you I like to be in control. I guess they're right. I like to arm myself with information, so I *know* what is going on around me and why.

By the time I was three, the meds they had put me on had strengthened my bones enough that I no longer needed leg braces, and the train trips to Philadelphia to visit the specialist became adventures. I still hated seeing the phlebotomist with her little tray of needles and vials. I would curl my fingertips inside my hands so she wouldn't see them and decide to prick me! But I thought X-rays were fun, trying to lie as still as I could while they took pictures of my bones. And Mom would take me out for pancakes after fasting bloodwork. I got a kick out of telling my friends I had an "incurable disease." They always look so shocked!

By the time I started college, they still didn't know much about my condition, which was then being called, "Vitamin D Resistant Rickets." But I was arming myself with knowledge in areas I *did* control. I think I was the only freshman at the state university that had the entire campus map memorized weeks before classes began! My peers thought I was an upperclassman because I could answer all their questions. Nope. I just read all the papers, including the entire catalog, cover to cover!

Years later, when my own son was diagnosed as an infant, the research had progressed to the more accurate description of X-Linked Hypophosphatemia. Real information was actually available! I finally sensed a bit of control over this very rare condition that in me, as in many of us, spontaneously developed, or, as in my son's case, was inherited.

I was grateful that hospital policies had changed in that generation, too. So grateful that I could stay with my son, at his bedside. Grateful that he would never fear I had abandoned him. Truth be told, he actually looked *forward* to his in-patient research weeks at our local hospital. (Now *that's* going a bit too far!) It was the only time he was allowed to play video-games. And every moment the Recreational Therapy department was open, he'd be there!

I am even more grateful for the current research and the clinical trials that are leading to an anti-FGF23 therapy that will provide better care for our children's children. Every time I see my specialist (yes, I'm still on meds, even though I'm now nearly sixty!) I ask about what's new with the research. I want to know what to expect as I age, and what my future grandchildren can anticipate, both good and bad.

I am especially grateful for The XLH Network, Inc. and the information it provides for us all, so we can *all* learn from the researchers and from each other. We don't need to feel helpless! We can *all* take control!

# XLH is Hard and Amazing
# by Raya Quereau

Having XLH can be hard and amazing. I'm nine now, and when I was seven I joined a pretend running group that a girl in my class made up. Some of the girls in the group called me slow and I didn't know why. Later I asked my dad why, and he said sometimes people with XLH get tired faster so it wasn't that I was slow.

Sometimes my friends even asked me why I take medicine. Sometimes I told them, sometimes I didn't.

By the time I was eight, I joined a group called Girls On The Run. This was not something my friends made up. One day my team was going to run a mock 5K and I ran the whole thing.

It can be hard to have XLH, but when you think about it, it is amazing. For example, I have a best friend I met because of XLH. We met on XLH Day. We see each other at the doctor's office sometimes, and once we even went to New York City together. Having XLH is amazing.

# The Glass is Half Full, Part One
# by Nancy J. Alauzen

As a naive teenager and young adult, I believed that XLH was single-dimensional and that by correcting the bowed deformities of my legs, all of my XLH issues would be conquered! Luckily wisdom comes with age. I soon realized that in addition to perfectly straight legs, other XLH issues needed to be managed simultaneously. I came to realize that my dental symptoms, hearing loss, new orthopedic challenges, and potential parathyroid surgery to regulate my parathyroid hormone levels all needed to be addressed. I had two choices on how I could manage these multiple challenges. I chose the "glass is half full" approach but not before realizing XLH was much more than correcting my severely bowed legs.

The compact, three-bedroom ranch house in suburban Pittsburgh, on a quiet dead end street, was a safe haven for me before starting school. While the family would expand in later years, before I started kindergarten, my mom, dad, younger brother and sister would travel to Sparrow Lake in Ontario, Canada. Those first five years were carefree. In addition to the enjoyable summer trips, our family would travel to see grandparents, aunts, uncles, cousins and family friends. The kids on my street developed a close bond and there were countless hours of fun and games.

Things changed when I started school. Until then, I didn't know I was different from any other kid. My parents, aunts, uncles, cousins and family friends never treated me differently. I was born with a metabolic bone disorder that was called Vitamin D Resistant Rickets and is now referred to as X-Linked Hypophosphatemia (XLH). The visual effects of XLH were very obvious: short stature, waddling gait, and severely bowed legs. My legs were bowed enough that you could put a basketball between them. One of the earlier corrections suggested to my parents was metal leg braces. The metal vertical bars extended from hip to ankle and were fastened with horizontal white leather straps. The braces were heavy, awkward, and not at all fashionable!

To this normally outgoing kid, with a constant smile, life became difficult when kids would point and say, "What's wrong with her?" and "Why does she walk so funny?" In the dimly lit gymnasiums in grade school and middle school, I tried to be patient as the sports captains chose their team members. The entire class assembled in a large circle and one by one everyone was chosen for a team. The group dwindled and by default the captain with the last choice chose me.

As surgical options to correct the bowing were presented to my parents and me, my major focus was to get a pair of surgically corrected straight legs to prepare for future knee replacements and to solve all of my XLH challenges forever. It soon became apparent the other important complications could not be ignored. These were medical issues needed attention. As these conditions surfaced, however, I realized that if I approached every aspect with a "glass half full" attitude and mentality I could manage my XLH successfully.

# Rare-Disease Children and Their Parents
# by Sheila G. Hunter

I do not have any children. For a brief moment in college after watching a movie in class about the wonders of childbirth, I thought that having a child might be cool since childbirth looked so amazing in the movie, but that was a short-lived thought. As a young adult, when I had a flicker of a thought about becoming a parent one day, I always reverted back to my childhood beliefs that there didn't need to be another kid in the world like me and that being the mother of a child with my medical challenges would be hard.

That's not to say that I had a miserable childhood. I don't think I did. I was a happy child who had many hobbies and interests, a loving immediate and extended family, and some close friends. But I was still a misfit.

My favorite childhood movie was *Rudolph the Red-Nosed Reindeer*, probably because I so identified with the toys on the Island of Misfit Toys. There were several reasons why I was a misfit. One reason was that I was very short and walked with a distinct waddle. Both of these characteristics were pointed out to me on a regular basis by kids in grade school and by friends who liked to pat me on the head, which I hated. It's been a while since I've been patted on the head—four years to be exact. I was fifty-two when that last happened, and

I'm still friends with that individual. Aging has a way of mellowing a person.

Although I don't have any children, I have pondered many times what my parents went through having a child with a rare bone disease. In 1961, when I was diagnosed at the age of one, XLH was called Vitamin D Resistant Rickets, and people only focused on the "rickets" part of the name. Because of this, some people were certain that my mother needed to give me more milk. It's not unusual, of course, for the most ignorant people to give out the most advice. And my mother got plenty of advice because there were a lot of ignorant people around back then. Today, thanks to Google, no one ever says ignorant things, right?

My parents had to take me for regular blood draws and X-rays to check my progress when I was a child because I was prescribed a "Vitamin D preparation," as my mother remembers it being called. My mother also had to exercise my legs and keep me from sitting improperly. I remember that I was not supposed to sit on the floor in a particular way, but I did anyway. I can't really describe that forbidden sitting position, but I can say that I wouldn't be able to sit like that now at the age of fifty-six! Those childhood years were the flexible years.

At the age of four, I was put in leg braces. The braces were state of the art leather and steel contraptions that look like some sort of punishment, if you ask me. I still have them. My mother tried to get rid of them once. When I was in high school, I found them in her pile of Goodwill donations in the trunk of the car. I rescued the braces, telling her that there was no way in the world anyone would want those. I didn't know in that moment what I would do with them, but I removed them from her trunk because I felt donating or keeping them was my decision to make, not hers. A short while later, I repurposed the braces for a "found object" sculpture I constructed in high school. I got some really strange looks from my classmates and my art teacher, but more important, I got an A for my project. One mom's tax deductible contribution became her daughter's improved grade-point average.

I still have my leg braces. I don't know what to do with them now. I fantasize that one day someone will create an orthopedic museum and donors from around the world will pull out these antiques and send them in as a testament to their childhood bone diseases and abnormalities. The plaque on my donated braces will say, "Sheila H. wore these from 1964-65 to assist in straightening out her bowed legs caused by X-Linked Hypophosphatemia. Though her legs are still bowed, these braces might have prevented them from being worse."

My grandmother used to tell me the story of the day I wore the braces for the first time. My parents dropped me off at Grandma's house while they ran an errand. Grandma told me that I just leaned back against the kitchen wall (and she'd point to the exact spot), and with "big ol' tears a-rollin' down your face," she said, "you slid down to the floor with those unbendable steel and leather contraptions and sat there and cried. So, I slid down to the floor, too, and cried with you." I still miss her, almost thirty years after her death.

My dad also told me recently that it was upsetting at first for him to watch me wear those braces. In fact, he wasn't sure I'd be able to walk in them. Then, not too long after getting them, I figured out how to run in them, he says. When he told me this story, I thought of Forrest Gump and the scene in that movie where he runs out of his leg braces. That scene made me cry when I watched that movie the first time.

I have few memories of wearing my braces. I remember scratching my little rocking chair with them (I still have that rocking chair), and I remember scratching the toilet seat with them. I also have some childhood photos of me wearing them. In one photo of me in the leg braces, I am wearing a frilly dress and my giant "Indian" headdress, and I am carrying a spear. It's obvious to me from that photo that I developed a strong sense of fashion at a very early age.

As I write this and think about this kid that I know from fifty-year-old photographs and from stories told to me by my family members, I wonder, "Would it have been so bad to have a kid like me?" I understand her now better than ever. I "get" her. My parents did not have any experience to help them deal with a child like me. I was a spontaneous case of XLH. In the 1960s there were no support groups to help parents navigate the health care system or deal with the emotional and psychological effects of having a child like me. Today's parents have many more resources available to help them deal with having a child with a rare disease.

But even with all these additional resources, parents today still experience fear and worry about their affected children. My parents worry about me even now. I feel for them and for parents today who have children with XLH. We now understand that XLH is not just a childhood disease. We know that there is a progression that goes with us into adulthood and can give parents a lifetime of worry.

So, it is primarily for the parents—my parents and others—that I have been involved in two XLH clinical studies. One was in 2014, and I am currently enrolled in another study. I realize that these studies may benefit me, but I also often think of today's parents, parents like mine who received the news that "something is wrong" with their baby. I especially sympathize with those whose child's XLH is caused by a spontaneous mutation. I have known other parents over the years who have dealt with an unexpected health challenge with their child and wondered, "What did we do wrong? Could we have prevented this?" Even though disabilities in biblical times were thought to have been caused by sin in the family, and we know better now, many people still have self-doubt. My mother even wondered if she was giving me enough milk even though I was not diagnosed with that type of rickets.

Enrolling in these XLH clinical studies allows me to contribute to the ongoing narrative of living with XLH. Today's children with XLH will have different stories than mine. Their stories won't be peppered with leg braces, countless surgeries, and dental procedures and with being made fun of in school or being the last one picked for the ball team. Today's children who are born with XLH will grow up with an effective treatment or maybe even with a cure. We are so close to finding the perfect treatment, and I am helping in my own "small" way (yes, pun intended) to contribute to this exciting future for families affected with XLH.

Do I regret not having children? No, I do not. I would have had to put myself in the very difficult position of making a personal decision about taking the chance of passing my XLH on to a child. I honestly don't know what I would have decided. The many good qualities I could have passed down (sense of humor, music and art ability, and thick hair with a little bit of wave to it but not too unruly) outweigh the negative side of having XLH. But I simply could not have made that decision when I was younger.

I have decided one thing though. Today's children with XLH are my children. Because of that, I will continue to submit myself to studies and surveys and other opportunities to help insure that their future will be as pain- and disability-free as possible.

# A Child of the Forties
# by Lorna Brandt

When I first started walking as a young child over seventy years ago (in the mid-1940s), it was evident to my parents and others that my legs were bowed more than what could initially be attributed to being in diapers. Neither of my parents had any problem with bowed legs, nor did my twin sister or our two older brothers. We lived on a farm, and I had access to plenty of milk and sunshine as recommended by a local doctor. Braces were used for a while when I was around two or three years old, but there was no improvement from their use.

My mother had a great positive attitude, and worked to instill that attitude in all of us kids. She had some big challenges of her own, and her attitude was to just do the best you can and then to deal with or accept what you can't change and get on with life. We were always taught to respect others and to treat others as we would want to be treated. I had a very supportive family, and I had a lot of extended family and friends in the area when growing up on the farm and in the small town where we moved after leaving the farm. In the lower grades in school, it was normal for me to be one of the *last* students chosen for teams to compete in outdoor activities because I wasn't very tall or fast or good at sports. However, when classmates chose students to team up with them for a *spelling bee*, I was one of the *first* ones chosen to be on a team because I was good at spelling. I always did enjoy learning but also was aware of being stared at, whether in school or shopping, or on vacation, and this continued somewhat here and there throughout life. There was really nothing one could do but try to ignore it (When he was much younger, my brother came up with the comment that "it doesn't take brains to stare.").

By the time I was seven, I had been seen at two different teaching hospitals, each around two hundred to three hundred miles from home, and this condition was just called rickets at that time. We didn't have a lot of savings or insurance for this but my parents did what they could to seek any necessary treatment. Shortly before my ninth birthday, I was seen at yet another facility further from home, and it was here where I underwent surgery for the first time. I had never been on any medications when they performed osteotomies on both lower legs to correct the bowing. I was in the hospital for most of the summer with casts on both legs and confined to my bed. It was a challenge to be in the hospital all summer, but I had support from back home with lots of get well cards and birthday cards. I also enjoyed many learning experiences including learning about medical and nursing care and the various tools and procedures used, as well as learning Bible stories and songs, reading books, and enjoying lots of special entertainment for the young patients in the hospital.

Visiting hours were very limited, so we learned to enjoy what was available around us and to appreciate seeing family during the few hours available one day a week. When the casts were removed, and I started walking again, there was unfortunately no improvement, and the legs eventually became even more bowed than prior to the surgery.

A few years later I was again seen by physicians at one of the teaching hospitals where I had been seen in earlier years. I was involved in some ongoing studies to find the reason for the rickets. Although it was recognized that this disorder was not because of lack of proper nutrition, the cause had not yet been identified. They eventually diagnosed me with Vitamin D Resistant Rickets and I was put on gradually increased doses of vitamin D until reaching 50,000 units a day. I remained on that for around four or five years. I was also told that they would not do any surgery until I reached the age when one would normally stop growing in height, sometime in the teen years. I do remember one instance of appearing before a room full of doctors in conference as they studied about this unusual condition. Standing on a little stage in front of all these doctors, I was dressed rather scantily, so that the students were better able to see any effects this disorder had on my spine and legs, as well as the less obvious deformities in my arms. It could have been a very embarrassing experience for me, but I was able to get through it by understanding that this was a learning experience for the doctors and hopefully it could be of great benefit in future treatment of children with this problem.

I was a junior in high school when I had surgery again with tibial and femoral osteotomies of each leg. The first leg was done in two separate procedures in January. After an osteotomy of the femur, I was put in traction for a few weeks. That was followed by an osteotomy of the tibia, after which I was put in a hip spika cast and could get up then and learn to walk with crutches or canes. The same was done with the second leg in two separate procedures in July of the same year. I remember attending our high school Junior Prom with the hip spika cast on, using canes for assistance in walking. The theme of the Prom that year was "Candyland," and I decorated my canes with red and white crepe paper to look like peppermint sticks. It certainly helped to bring some enjoyment and acceptance of the situation for me, and there were many fun comments and smiles from classmates. The result of these surgeries was very good, and for the first time in my life I had *straight* legs.

# Busted, With a Capital B
# by Gini Patrick

The summer of 1966 I met Lucinda, who forever changed my way of looking at life. She was a "bad girl" in the eyes of many adults and truly a force to be reckoned with in mine. In short, I adored her.

When I was admitted to the hospital that summer, Lucinda was the first person I encountered on the ward. "Get anything good?" she asked as she hopped up on my bed. You see, whenever new patients came onto the ward, they had a duffel bag full of donated gifts waiting for them on their newly assigned bed.

Lucinda and I were both nine years old that summer. She was from the big city of Cincinnati, Ohio and I was from a small rural town in Indiana, called Windfall. As black and white as two people get, we were like yin and yang, balancing each other out perfectly. Our friendship became rock solid within a matter of hours. From that point on we went everywhere together, holding hands as young girls often do, sharing secrets, and finding security in our bond as "best friends" on the ward.

There was one nurse who was generally disliked by both patients and staff. Her name was Miss B—, and she was tall, skinny, gray-haired, and mean. She was known for being a grump and for doing things like handing out cold wash cloths in the morning to clean our sleepy eyes with, even though all the other nurses made sure to hand out steaming hot ones. It was as if she *always* woke up on the wrong side of the bed. That's how we saw it anyway, and Lucinda had a plan to get her out of our hair once and for all. Because I was her friend and confidante, she told only me of her *coup de grace* that would bring down the evil Miss B— . Knowing I would not betray her, Lucinda let me in on every detail, and thinking it sounded like the perfect crime, I swore allegiance to help her as best I could.

The first task at hand was to somehow pilfer magic markers, scissors, and contact paper from Occupational Therapy, commonly referred to as OT. Easier said than done, since this meant sneaking off the ward unnoticed, and then navigating the long hallway to the OT room without being discovered by any of the staff. We decided the time period between dinner and evening snack, or "nutrition" as the nurses called it, would be best. While I stood guard, Lucinda tiptoed down to OT and disappeared inside. Although it was probably only a few minutes, it felt like an eternity before she stuck her head out the door to check if the halls were empty. I gave her the "all clear" signal by scratching the top of my head and she suddenly emerged. As she approached me I was shocked by how much stuff she had in her arms and immediately began to panic about getting caught. Seeing the fear in my eyes, Lucinda quickly shoved the contact paper under my dress, the markers and scissors up her sleeves, and we were off in a flash. As we rounded the nurses' station my heart was thumping and my face was on fire, but no one said a word. We headed straight for the sunroom on the far end of the ward where we could work in privacy. Phase one of our scheme had been a smashing success!

Honing in on my artistic skills, Lucinda decided she should cut the brightly colored contact paper into wide strips, like bumper stickers, while I used the markers to inscribe them with various slogans aimed against Miss B—. Recently, many of the older girls on the ward had resorted to calling her "BB" behind her back. Upon inquiry, I had been told this stood for Bitchy B—. Even though we weren't quite sure what that meant, Lucinda and I knew it wasn't *good*, so our first slogan read; "Down with Bitchy B—!" This was quickly followed by "BB Go Home!" and "BB Should Retire!" I decorated the bumper stickers with daisies, which Lucinda then colored in, and we both worked feverishly until we had finished about a dozen or so. At this point we were starting to lose daylight, which meant snacks would soon be served, and we had to clean up and get to our beds so as not to arouse suspicion. I hid our work behind a row of *Nancy Drew* mysteries on one of the bookshelves in the sunroom, and we agreed to sneak back later that night when the nurses were on break to complete our dastardly deed. We headed back to the ward, giggling to ourselves conspiratorially, quickly choosing which walls to plaster our stickers on.

Naturally, Miss B— was handing out snacks that night. As she rolled the cart full of bananas, graham crackers, and apple juice down the aisle, I found I couldn't even look at her for fear of giving away our secret plans. Likewise, Lucinda couldn't look at me either, but did manage a long hissing "shhhhhhh" as Miss B— approached our beds.

"What's wrong with you two tonight? Cat got your tongues?" she asked as her blue-veined hands thrust tiny glasses of juice towards our faces.

We took our "nutrition" in silence, then walked hand in hand to brush our teeth and put on our PJs. Neither of us spoke a word as TV-time ended, lights-out came, and everyone went to bed. I remember lying in the dark, pretending to sleep, but thinking all we had to do was wait until the coast was clear……

Looking back on it all now, I'm not really sure *how* we got caught. I mean, we had been sooooo careful! All I know is, one minute I'm standing on a chair peeling off the backing to a piece of contact paper, and the next minute lights are coming on, two nurses are chasing Lucinda right behind me, and she's yelling at the top of her lungs, "Run for yer life!" We were busted with a capital B!

*Editors' note: This is a much-condensed excerpt from Gini Patrick's memoir,* On the Ward: Tales from a Children's Hospital*, available at major online booksellers.*

# Resilience Through Adversity
# by Kaggy Dale

When I was around three or four, the doctors decided to break my lower legs and reset them straight. With gut-wrenching clarity I remember Mum leaving me with these strangers in white uniforms and funny hats. I watched her walk away and didn't see her again for days. Mum didn't drive, she didn't have access to handy public transport, and Dad was busy working, so she couldn't visit me during the week. I had to wait those long, lonely days until the weekend when Dad and Mum could visit. The feeling of waking up after surgery alone, vomiting violently and in extreme pain without my Mum will never leave my subconscious. I'm sure that the isolation and abandonment that I experienced then affects me and my problems trusting people to this day. Some say that I am very independent and self-reliant now; well, that's because I learnt very young that I had to be. I had no choice.

I became very self-conscious about going out in public and the thought of walking around in the streets was unbearable. Whenever I went out with my family, I'd walk behind them so that I wouldn't be seen, and I could avoid the stares. When I was a naive youngster, I was so uninhibited and didn't realise that those who stared at me in the street were being critical, so I would just smile back and go on my merry way. Sometimes they'd say something sarcastic to Mum and because I didn't really understand their remarks, I thought they were just being friendly, but after the age of about eight I knew better. Those old familiar sarcastic remarks about diet and sunshine would resurface repeatedly. In their ignorance these critics thought I had common 'lack of sunshine or Vitamin D' rickets, and to this day that word *rickets* annoys the hell out of me. At the time I didn't consider how Mum must have felt, I only thought about how bad I felt. It must have been so awful for her because it happened time and time again no matter where we went.

Other boys at school cruelly started calling me X-legs, because I had a habit of standing with my legs crossed-over thinking it would make the bowing less obvious. Frankly, I would resort to anything to camouflage myself, like standing behind walls, poles, or chairs or sitting for as long as possible. When sitting I looked quite acceptable, so I sat a lot. Walking across a large room in front of people was something I avoided at all costs because every eye in the room would be on my legs. I'd saunter around the perimeter of a room to get to the other side. Sport at school was so embarrassing because I waddled like a duck when I ran and all the kids would laugh, so I just gave up.

Finally I'd had enough and wanted to be like my sister and brother and everybody else in the world. I wanted my legs fixed no matter what had to be done. My severe bandyness was dominating my peace of mind and affecting my entire life. I was constantly pre-occupied with other people's legs, all those normal legs everywhere, and I'd never ever seen anyone else with legs like mine anywhere. It was like trying to find a four-leafed clover. The thought of another operation was scary but I wanted my abnormality to disappear.

The hospital visits were really embarrassing for me as the doctors and students would stare, poke, prod, measure, photograph, analyse, and ask lots of questions making me feel like a guinea-pig. Finally, it was concluded that they could not straighten my legs again until I'd finished growing. My hopes of being normal were dashed for years and I was devastated, but basically I knew I had no choice but to get on with my life, crooked legs and all. My resilience was being formed during those years of adversity, and the coping skills I developed then would serve me well in the years to come. God knows I'd need them.

When young I was preoccupied with the negative impact my medical condition had on my life, but now, as a life-experienced adult, I realise I owe everything to it. I hope at long last I can look upon my XLH without bitterness, and I guess the tragedy is not what I've suffered, but perhaps only what I've missed which isn't that much in the scheme of things. All those ordeals actually enhanced my perceptions of life and people, definitely helping me make better choices and giving me strength, and what I've learned from the people around me has enhanced my life immeasurably.

*Editors' note: This is a much-condensed excerpt from Kaggy Dale's as-yet-unpublished memoir,* Bent, But Not Twisted. *We hope you'll have the opportunity to read the full life story someday.*

# Someone Who Understands
# by Bess Thomason Smith

I'm one of the lucky ones. I say that not because I suffer any less than other people with XLH, but because I had a comrade in this fierce battle growing up. My sister, Mallorie Kate, and I were both diagnosed with XLH in 1994. Just like every individual who has been diagnosed with XLH, we were, and continue to be, warriors. We persevered through the fiery pain, and we faced challenges that no child, nor any adult for that matter, should ever have to face.

Up until the ages of nine and ten, we had both been told that we were simply born bow-legged and would eventually grow out of it. Years passed, corrective surgeries were done, and braces were worn. But no local doctor was familiar with the metabolic disease that ravaged our bones, and my parents did the best they could to create a sense of normalcy in our lives.

Being born in the South, we were accustomed to boisterous people who had little reserve when it came to voicing their opinions about our unusual outward appearance. It was difficult to fight back the tears.

However, as fate would have it, we were discovered during a shopping trip at Walmart. A Shriners member, who voluntarily transported children in need to a Shriners Hospital, saw the two of us struggling to walk the store with our mother and introduced himself. At that moment, our journey into the unknown world of Hypophosphatemia began.

Grade school was grueling. Between long trips to endocrinologists' offices, health monitoring, scheduled medications, more surgeries, and trips to the Shriners Hospital, it was tough being a kid. How does a child explain the deep ache of constant bone pain to an adult? All we could say was that it always hurt. Pep rallies, dances, recess, and even sitting in desks was painful.

Mallorie Kate loved playing basketball, yet there were many times I could see tears flowing amidst the perspiration. We even joined our school's show choir just to prove that we could sing and dance with the cool kids. I was a shy adolescent, but Mallorie voiced her frustrations. I remember her cursing and crying out in pain as we practiced our steps in front of large mirrors.

Being eighteen months apart in age, we shared a close bond. We both truly knew how the other one felt. It hurt not being normal. Fitting in was a constant struggle.

At that point in my life, I did not realize how much more blessed I was than other people suffering from XLH. Even though I was physically crippled, I was not alone. I had a comrade. I had someone to relate to and who understood my pain. Unfortunately, Mallorie Kate was involved in a fatal 3-wheeler accident in 1998, and I found myself coming of age without my confidante. I was brokenhearted.

XLH is not merely a painful disease, but a state of forlornness and loneliness. No one truly knows how you feel, and you can't fully explain it.

Now that I'm an educator in my thirties, I've learned to use XLH as a stepping stone to grasp opportunities and positively influence others, especially children. I can be relatable to the unrelatable and reach the unreachable child in the classroom at school. My bones may be crippled, but my heart is so full that it spills out into the little lives I teach each day. What a privilege to set an example in such a way!

# The Sibling Experience
# by Marah Inman

"She will walk like this," I explained to my friends. I bent my legs slightly, pushed them apart, and began to walk to illustrate my sister's movements. Looking back to this moment in the second grade, I realize several different things. Most importantly, I was coming across as an unconcerned and terrible big sister. And in some ways, my sister might have thought I was unintentionally making fun of her rare disorder (and inaccurately at that). I believe I have become a much more empathetic "role model" since then.

Ever since I can remember, XLH is just something Sanders has had. Until recently, I never truly understood what my sister having a rare bone disease meant. For a long time, all I understood about XLH was that Sanders took medicine in her chocolate milk, was shorter than other people, and got to go on "fun" trips to Yale with my parents. However, real life turned out not to be that simple. Having XLH means that my strong willed, sassy little sister is going to have a harder time with simple things that I take for granted.

One thing most people do not understand is the jealousy that comes with being the sibling of anyone with a disease that somehow makes them "special." Even though it is negative attention in the sense that we all want to just be normal, it is still attention in the eyes of a kid. Any trip, even if it is to the doctor, is a special adventure with mom and dad. I was always jealous of the new friends she got to make, restaurants where she got to eat, and her opportunities to experience new environments and places. It is hard to understand that while all these things are fun, they come after blood draws, finger pricks, physical therapy, and shots. This feeling is completely normal, and I just want other siblings of XLH patients to know that this is a normal feeling. I still get jealous of the attention my sister gets, but I also realize that we, as an entire family, are making a difference and that my sister is here to support me too.

# TRANSITION TO ADULTHOOD

## The Science

At present, there is no official "standard of care" for XLH adults, and there is some controversy with respect to whether the treatment with phosphorus and activated vitamin D causes more harm than good. Many teens are dismissed from care when their growth plates close. There appears to be a consensus that treatment benefits may outweigh risks when 1) the patient is experiencing significant pain, or 2) the patient is preparing for or recovering from orthopedic surgery.

When treated in adulthood, XLH patients are seen by endocrinologists (specialists dealing with the endocrine system and hormones), their blood is tested for levels of phosphorus (among other things), and they may be x-rayed for evidence of osteomalacia (soft/weak bones in adults).

Specific treatment methods may vary depending on the severity and complications of each individual case. At present, treatment requires a delicate balance of activated vitamin D (calcitriol) and oral phosphate (such as K-Phos or Neutra-Phos). Treatment must be monitored by a clinician to minimize the consequences of treatment, including secondary hyperparathyroidism, hypercalcemia and nephrocalcinosis.

Often the early adulthood years are relatively free of any change in noticeable symptoms, such as pain or calcifications, although the low blood phosphorus levels remain.

For more information, the journal article, A Clinician's Guide to X-Linked Hypophosphatemia, is a good start. You can read it here: https://www.ncbi.nlm.nih.gov/pmc/articles/PMC3157040/.

In addition, XLH patients may experience a variety of dental issues during their twenties, most notably frequent spontaneous abscesses in the absence of trauma or cavities.

# On Becoming a Mother
# by Kimberly Murray

I'M PREGNANT! My husband and I were so happy to hear this news after trying for five years. XLH was not the cause of the delay. My husband's sperm didn't know how to swim in a straight line.

And then, reality sets in. I'M PREGNANT. With XLH.

I was always told any children I have will have a fifty percent chance of inheriting it. Okay. No problem. This won't happen to me. I have been through enough with four surgeries, years of physical therapy, general counseling, and daily pain.

Madelyn Marie was born on December 15th, 2015. My perfect little baby was here and she was just like me in every way! Feisty, strong-willed, and she knows what she wants. On June 17th, 2016 we received the genetics report back that she did in fact inherit XLH from me. I spent a total of three hours hysterically crying (the ugly kind of crying, Kim Khardashian style) and feeling sorry for myself. Then my mom said the one thing I needed to hear: "If anyone is capable of taking care of Madelyn, it's you. You will know what do for her. God made you her mother for a reason." And she was right. So very right. Before the end of the day, I had an appointment set up for Madelyn to get things started for her treatment. I was already a member of The XLH Network, Inc. so I jumped online and started diving into the forum, looking for anything related to XLH and babies/children. I have learned so much in the past year about my disease thanks to the Network. Also, for the first time in my thirty-four years of living, I actually got to meet others with this same disease. I never would have thought that was possible.

Life with XLH has taught me so much. My appreciation for the little things in life, my optimism, my patience, my compassion for others. These are things I will teach my daughter. She is my angel, the love of my life. And she is literally the happiest baby I have ever known! She wakes up with a smile on her face and goes to sleep smiling. I plan to make sure she stays this happy—every day. XLH is only one small part of us. It does not define us.

Someone once said, "You were given this life because you are strong enough to live it." Agreed!

# The Person I Am Today
# by Latrell Castanon

After I turned eighteen and was released from the Shriners Hospital, I, for the most part, tried to ignore that I had anything wrong with me. XLH was not about to let that happen, and during my first pregnancy, I had my first bout with abscessed teeth. I suppose my body was unable to handle the amount of phosphorus or Vitamin D the baby was taking from me. Either way, it was not good. I came to find out that my teeth would be a serious issue for the rest of my life. I never had a cavity, but I had abscesses. How does that happen? The culprit, defective dentin in my teeth from, guess what, XLH.

During my pregnancies in my twenties I was put on Rocaltrol, though there isn't much information on how safe it is, and both of my children were born healthy. I was told that a C-section would be required for both kids because of my ischial spines in the pelvis being too close together, though I don't know if that is true.

It wasn't until 2001 that I would find out that I was not just okay and as normal as I wanted to be. My husband, kids and I had moved back to West Texas and I was working at the hospital on the Orthopedic floor and noticed that my lower back was aching pretty regularly. I went ahead and scheduled an appointment with a primary care provider and went in for my initial visit. I mentioned that I had XLH and told her about the pain.

She seemed to think the fact that it was "banding pain" was significant, so I agreed to get an MRI. I then went back to work where I attempted to lift a bilateral amputee by myself and was then completely out of commission. On the same day, I received a call about my MRI. I needed to be referred to an orthopedic surgeon because the MRI showed absolute stenosis in the L3-S1 region. Of course workers compensation was not thrilled that the back injury had aggravated my stenosis. They refused to acknowledge that it wasn't muscle spasms. Some of the treatment that they prescribed, such as traction, actually continued to worsen the symptoms. I fought for two years, but I eventually had surgery to remove the excess bone. It helped tremendously with the pain, and I was able to get around better. I have continued to have issues stemming from osteochondral defects in the joints, enthesopathy, and osteosclerosis.

During my ordeal with the back problems and surgery, I became an amateur XLH detective. I used to call it Vitamin D Resistant Rickets, but after becoming a member of The XLH Network, Inc., I found out it is called X-linked Hypophosphatemia. The Network has been instrumental in assisting me with information and support through the years. There has been a increase in information and outreach regarding how the disease affects adults. There is a wealth of information on the comorbid conditions in adults with XLH, and questions are still being asked regarding the need for continued treatment with medications.

I truly feel like I wouldn't be the person I am today if it hadn't been for XLH. It has made me more compassionate and has definitely kept me humbler than I would have been without it. It is true that I have weak bones, but thank God for the strong will, as it certainly is a requirement of an XLH life.

# Over Forty-Five Years of Clinical Trials
# by Geoff Edelson

I was born in 1958 and diagnosed before 1960, practically unheard of for spontaneous cases of XLH at the time. And I've been in clinical trials ever since I can remember.

I participated in my first clinical trial when I was eleven. Up to that point I was on the common medicinal protocol of the time. I don't remember what the protocol was exactly, but I know I was taking dramatic amounts of vitamin D. That first trial involved six different month-long stays over a three-year period in the Clinical Research Center (CRC) at the Hospital of the University of Pennsylvania. My dad had to work, and my mom was home with my three brothers, the youngest of whom was two at the time I started. I stayed at the hospital by myself each time, and they returned to our home in northern New Jersey, not far from New York City.

I have a few salient memories from those hospital visits. I turned thirteen during this trial, so I was preparing to become Bar Mitzvah up to the event itself. The University of Pennsylvania rabbi came to the hospital and worked with me at least twice each week to help in the preparation for this important event. My parents visited me at least one day each weekend and brought my school assignments with them. I then dutifully sent my completed work back with them. I guess you could say that I basically taught myself.

My cousins grew up in the Washington, DC area and I had a close friend at the time who lived just outside Baltimore. They, along with my parents and brothers, all visited me one weekend each month. Those weekends were always a big deal because the hospital let me leave the premises as long as I came back for meals, tests, and, of course, collections. The down side of those excursions was going out for meals and watching them eat. I was only allowed to eat what they served me at the hospital because they were monitoring my intakes. I had to lick my plate clean after every meal! Another fond memory is going to University of Pennsylvania home basketball games at the Palestra with my doctors. To this day I remain close with one of them.

Not surprisingly, the hospital staff had to work hard to keep me entertained. Ultimately, they had to let me go to the physical therapy facility so I could work out and burn off energy. I was pretty athletic at the time and would work out vigorously while other patients were struggling to rehabilitate themselves. It was an important reminder of just how fortunate I was in spite of my rare disorder. There was also a girl, younger than me, who was in the trial as well. We raced wheelchairs up and down the halls of the adults-only CRC. I don't remember her name, but she was the only other person with XLH that I would meet until I entered my fifties.

I participated in a few other trials between then and the current KRN23/burosumab trial. One trial took place while I was in college, and I remember that was really the first time my friends had any idea that I had a rare disease. Some of them made the trip from Dartmouth in New Hampshire to Yale in Connecticut to visit me. I was also in a trial with my daughter over fifteen years ago. That's an interesting story for another time because she doesn't have XLH!

Finally, for the past six years, I've participated in the KRN23/burosumab trials for what researchers (and all of us!) hope will be the most promising therapy developed for the XLH community.

Recently, a friend asked me why I agreed to spend a significant portion of my life in these research trials. My parents influenced me significantly. My brothers and I were all raised with an emphasis on the importance of doing things in our own lives that would also benefit others. I remember my parents sitting me down and telling me of this opportunity to learn more about my disease (which, at the time, we called Vitamin D Resistant Rickets) and to contribute to what doctors knew about the disease so that I and others with the same condition would hopefully someday benefit. But they always told me it was, in the end, my decision.

After I elected to participate in that first trial, the rest were no-brainers. There was some hesitation that first time, but I am never hesitant now. I suppose that in some ways these trials are one of the ways that I have chosen to give to those in our community. I have spent over forty-five years in clinical trials, and I now know this means I have played a small part in this important work.

# An Addendum to Forty-Five Years of Clinical Trials
# by Joyce Olewski Inman

My daughter was diagnosed with XLH when she was two and a half years old. Our experiences with the XLH community have been the most rewarding of my life, and after reading Geoff's story about his experiences in clinical trials, I feel compelled to write an addendum of sorts to his narrative.

I met Geoff six years ago. We were already working together through our volunteer work with The XLH Network, Inc., but I met him in person on a cold day in Boston. I was attending a conference in the city, and he offered to come meet me for breakfast one morning. We had breakfast and talked for an hour or so, but my most significant memory from that morning involved walking away with the realization that my daughter had a full and wonderful future in front of her. Yes, there would be difficulties, but I realized after meeting Geoff that those difficulties did not need to stop her from doing any of the things she wanted to try.

Fast forward to a few years later. Our family was considering whether we should participate in a clinical trial. We knew that the trial medication had the potential to be life-changing, but that did not alter the fact that we would be traveling across the country constantly and that my daughter would be something of a guinea pig. I do not remember how or when I expressed my anxieties to Geoff, but I do remember him calling me to talk. And in that phone call, he asked me to let him go to lunch with my daughter so he could talk to her "from one spontaneous case to another" about what it means to be the only person in your family to have a rare disease and what it means to participate in a clinical trial.

I will never forget him reaching out to me and my family that year, and because I know Geoff's story, I will never forget that his experiences as a child helped lead to my daughter's initial successful treatments. Nor will I forget that because of his friendship and mentoring, my daughter's experiences might provide other families with similar moments of relief and opportunity.

# Life's Lively Lemons
# by Bryan from Missouri

I was doing well in college. I kept up a perfect grade-point average, completed my university honors requirements and community service hours in half the normal time, and was a respected officer in several student organizations, but still I had no idea what path I would pursue in life. I could have graduated after only three years with a BS in Computer Science but chose to add a second major and a minor to delay that day of reckoning another two semesters while also increasing my resume.

I had long been interested in artificial intelligence. Growing up, my trouble typically was that I wanted to learn and understand everything—the freedom of my home-school education allowed me to pursue an odd assortment of extracurricular activities ranging from robotics to videography to historical dance. Ever since I was five, however, I remember dreaming of creating creative human-level artificial minds with which to futurize the world, yet this goal was so deep an enigma that I had for many years abandoned hope of its pursuit. Around the end of my third undergraduate year, however, unexpected circumstances plowed a path into that mystery and renewed my passion for its study.

My troubles started when I was eighteen with general aches and fatigue. By my second year in college I could barely walk. My third year was characterized by a ceaseless intensifying headache which hindered concentration and sleep. I was born with XLH, inherited from my mother, and diagnosed in early infancy. All my life I'd enjoyed the care of doctors in my hometown who specialized in this rare bone disease, and beyond the characteristic symptom of bowed legs and short stature I grew up the picture of health and vitality such that I have never considered my XLH a disability, and do not to this day.

But at the commencement of my college years, by which time I had stopped growing, the medical researchers I'd worked with since birth and I agreed to cease all treatment, and my true adventure began. As stated, it began with fatigue, but quickly progressed beyond what was considered normal for XLH adults without medication. I never particularly experienced bone pain, and as such my doctors were reticent to blame my bone disease, but most every other part of me felt like it was falling apart and dying—joints, flesh, and especially my mind. The immobility and immobilizing headache from this mishap indirectly impacted the way I formed thoughts, rapidly restructuring my active consciousness from unified and engaged to abstract and modular, and choosing which mental faculties to animate or let rest required continuous conscious effort. But while the experience was harrowing, much good came from it as well. It greatly strengthened my trust in God for provision and life throughout each day's trials, and more peculiarly led to shaping what would also become my career at large.

For my own understanding's sake, and for the sake of the challenge, I put the measurable change within my own consciousness to use, gradually composing a model of the mind and a blueprint of creative intelligence through study and experience. It started as a casual way of passing time, but with progress came serious interest and fascination. After a few years, the model that resulted, though perhaps far from its goal, revealed to me that artificial thought may not be so far out of reach after all. But I also knew it would require extensive formal research and study.

Adversity matured curiosity into a sincere desire to continue the pursuit of cognitive artificial intelligence at the next level. Though my undergraduate school offered few research opportunities, I was able to gain experience and be admitted into a top research graduate program, where I now pursue a Ph.D. in artificial intelligence, developing cognitive architectures. The more I have studied, the greater appreciation I have gained for those gifts we are normally blessed to only see externally and for the clockwork we have always been free to take for granted. I still believe in pursuing that model, and it continues to grow and evolve with life's experiences.

Someone once said, "When life gives you lemons, eat them quickly before it takes them back again!" The troubles which spurred me down the study of artificial cognition did not last forever. Halfway through my junior year the decision was made to renew my medication. Most of my troubles ended within a few months' time, but the insights and curiosities they afforded me remain as compelling as ever. Creating lifelike behavior drew me to my chosen line of work, but it is that cross-sectional glimpse at life's union of body and mind and its given ability to create that presses me to further study.

Not all remnants of those rougher days have healed, and I will likely carry some of it for the rest of my life. But I would not be where I am today without both the good times and the bad, and if not for the patience, love, and care of the family and doctors God placed in my life. I especially would not be who I am today if not for XLH. And that, I believe, is a good thing.

# Then and Now
# by Rachael Jones

When I was growing up, there was little research and information readily available about XLH, and even less was known when my mother was diagnosed in her childhood. My mother (a spontaneous case) passed it on to both of her children (my brother and I). Other than the many doctor appointments, XLH was not something that we talked about in my family.

As a child, I didn't understand much about XLH other than that it caused me pain and kept me from growing very tall. My shorter stature is really what caused me the most frustration. I hated going into public places and having people stare and laugh at me. School too was awful at times. I couldn't participate in physical education classes like the other kids because I was either in too much pain or was much slower than the others. It was difficult dealing with physical education teachers who just assumed that I was making excuses and that I wasn't trying very hard, because they couldn't "see" anything wrong with me.

I desperately tried to separate myself from XLH. I wanted to be known for more than my aches and pains and short stature. I worked really hard in school because it was something that I could control and could actually do well. I also really loved dance. Even though I could never be a professional dancer, it didn't keep me from dancing. I started when I was two and have been dancing for fun ever since. However, I have injured my knees many times while dancing and have had several knee surgeries as a result. I have since learned to do different types of dance that are less strenuous on my knees, and I have learned how to listen to my body and to rest.

Once I became a parent, the way I viewed XLH changed. It was something I could no longer ignore. My husband and I decided that we needed to learn everything we could and to work to give our children the best medical care possible. I began researching XLH and was so happy to find The XLH Network, Inc. It was such a blessing to find research, information on XLH, and a group of people that knew what it was like to live with XLH.

As a parent, I am vigilant about keeping up on the latest research, finding qualified doctors with knowledge of XLH, and making sure that my kids do not miss medication doses. Most importantly, I hope to teach my children how to deal with the teasing they will experience throughout their lives. When I go to pick up my kids from school, there are children who laugh at me and call me names because I am short. My children are watching how I deal with it. When they look at me, I hope that they see someone who stands with grace amid adversity. However, I also hope that I can be honest with them that though I don't focus on the teasing, it still hurts. I want them to feel that they can be honest with me about their feelings as well. I want them to feel supported by me. I also want to teach them to be compassionate toward those who are different and to stand up for those who are being ostracized or mocked by others. It is my hope that my children grow up to be strong-willed, confident, and compassionate because of their experiences with XLH.

# I Go Through Life with Confidence by Rustam Zinnatullin

When I started to walk, I had a leg deformity. These same deformities of legs and low growth has my mother.

Until the age of seven, I was treated with the diagnosis of chondrodysplasia. At seven I was diagnosed with low phosphorus in the blood and hyperphosphaturia. I received treatment with vitamin D. I was seven times conducted operations on the leg bones. At age twenty-six, I found a doctor in Moscow, Kristina Kulikova. She found a mutation of PHEX gene and established the diagnosis XLH.

Since childhood I am an active lifestyle, engage in professional sports power lifting. In 2015 I became a world champion in the bench press with a barbell (Ekaterinburg, Russia). I have the title of master of sports of international class. Every day I have many hours of coaching.

In addition, I have finished two college of Radio Electronics, am currently studying at the Kazan National Research Technical University named after Tupolev, specialty "radio engineering," and lead the scientific work in the field of acoustic vibrations. I have a girlfriend, with whom I will soon start a family.

I consider myself a strong and successful young man, and I go through life with confidence no matter what happens.

## **Stares**
## **by Chris Younger**

All my life I've been getting stares,
You would think at this point I wouldn't care.

Vertically challenged at five-foot, zero inches,
Funny how the world lets you know you're different.

I traveled around and the stares are the same,
Whether in France, Costa Rica, Ireland, or Spain.

Kids are the best, stopping dead in their tracks,
Mouth wide open and pointing, "Mommy, look at
that."

Adults think they are better at giving the stare,
As I walk by you, yes I'm aware.

I can feel the presence, I can feel the dread,
And I catch you all the time with a quick turn of my
head.

On a good day I can laugh off a few,
But then there are times when I just say F-U.

There are times I think it would be great,
To wear a shirt with big letters saying I HAVE XLH.

And I'm not a dwarf or a little person, you see,
Just someone with too much circulating FGF23.

What amazes me most is when people strive for stares,
With piercings, or tattoos, or blue or green hair.

Maybe if they could walk in my shoes for a day,
They would appreciate normal, and how normal is OK.

And one day a year I have my way,
To blend in and not be different, and that's XLH Day.

So next time you dare to stare, be aware, and let me share,

That person knows, that person cares.

# LATER YEARS

## The Science

As mentioned above, there is, at present, no official "standard of care" for XLH adults, and there is some controversy with respect to whether the treatment with phosphorus and activated vitamin D causes more harm than good. Many teens are dismissed from care when their growth plates close. There appears to be a consensus that treatment benefits may outweigh risks when 1) the patient is experiencing significant pain, or 2) the patient is preparing for or recovering from orthopedic surgery.

When treated in adulthood, XLH patients are seen by endocrinologists (specialists dealing with the endocrine system and hormones), their blood is tested for levels of phosphorus (among other things), and they may be x-rayed for evidence of osteomalacia (soft/weak bones in adults).

Specific treatment methods may vary depending on the severity and complications of each individual case. At present, treatment requires a delicate balance of activated vitamin D (calcitriol) and oral phosphate (such as K-Phos or Neutra-Phos). Treatment must be monitored by a clinician to minimize the potential consequences of treatment, including secondary hyperparathyroidism, hypercalcemia and nephrocalcinosis.

Beginning as early as the late twenties, especially if treatment was discontinued, adults with XLH may find that their bone pain recurs, and they may begin to be aware of osteoarthritis from misaligned joints, occurring much earlier than in the general population. They may also experience widespread calcifications of soft tissue in the spine and weight-bearing joints, which affects mobility and range of motion.

For more information, the journal article, "A Clinician's Guide to X-Linked Hypophosphatemia," is a good start. You can read it here: https://www.ncbi.nlm.nih.gov/pmc/articles/PMC3157040/.

In addition, older XLH patients may continue to experience a variety of dental issues, most notably frequent spontaneous abscesses in the absence of trauma or cavities.

## Mrs. Smith's Bones Are Sick!
## by Bess Thomason Smith

"Mrs. Smith's bones are sick!" is usually how my second-grade students explain to a newcomer or younger children why their teacher is extremely short and bow legged. My awkward gait and deformities tend to catch kids (and most adults) off guard; but once they enter my classroom and "my world," we develop an enduring bond. It opens the door for daily teachable moments on acceptance, empathy, tolerance, humility, and love.

I honestly never thought I'd reach my tenth year as an elementary educator due to the chronic pain and difficulty being on my feet. I've learned that XLH impacts the mind, heart, and soul as well as the body. However, this disease doesn't have to debilitate my impact on precious children. I teach in a low socioeconomic area. XLH makes me relevant and relatable in a society where kids tend to feel unaccepted, pressured, and bullied.

Though I have physical weaknesses, I find strength in building up young lives for greatness.

# Long-Term Consequences of Treatment, Anonymous

When I was a kid in the 1950s, doctors thought that XLH, then known as Vitamin D Resistant Rickets (VDRR), was caused by a "resistance" to absorption of vitamin D. The theory was that if patients were given enough vitamin D—for me 50,000 units a day, a dosage that would horrify doctors today—enough would be absorbed to improve our bones.

The endocrinologist who treated me at a major medical center back then told my parents to "just keep giving her the vitamin D until she quits eating." That was the thinking of the day, that it wouldn't harm someone with VDRR—but my folks were told to keep in mind that loss of appetite is a symptom of overdose, so get a blood test if that happens. I can remember school pictures in which my skin looked really chalky; I'm sure I was in overdose then. When I was sixteen I had my osteotomies, and I was told to stop the vitamin D a couple of weeks before surgery and wouldn't need any treatment afterward since I "was grown."

About fifteen years later a specialist treating my children urged me to be treated, thinking everyone with it should be. I tried in vain to locate an endocrinologist who knew something about the condition, but even finding one for children was next to impossible. In several places we lived the labs didn't (and wouldn't, despite my requesting them to) even include the higher pediatric "normal" for phosphorus on their lab report form, which the pediatricians relied on. One doctor asked me what made me think my sons had XLH since their phosphorus level was "normal" (normal only for the adult reference range shown, and at that only with treatment). I was dumbfounded to think these pediatricians didn't even know what was normal for the children in their care.

It wasn't until I was about forty that I heard there was an endocrinologist in my new city who actually had adult XLH patients and knew how to treat them. I decided to see him, and he ordered the standard blood and urine testing before putting me on the newer treatment of phosphate and calcitriol. My creatinine clearance (a measurement of kidney function) in those first test results was quite a bit below normal, indicating chronic kidney disease. XLH kidney function is essentially normal, aside from something in our blood causing them to waste phosphorus. Excessive doses of vitamin D can damage the kidneys, though, so after the treatment of the 50s and 60s I was probably lucky my kidney function wasn't even worse.

Research articles now point out that a possible consequence of the phosphate treatment (at least if treatment is not balanced properly), and even to having XLH with or without treatment, is damage to the parathyroid glands. My parathyroid hormone level (PTH) was high-normal from the time I first saw this specialist, and in my mid-fifties it suddenly began to rise. Dosage adjustments kept it somewhat stable for a while, but eventually it rose much higher and my bone pain became so severe I wound up needing to use a walker to get around, while previously I had managed to get around without any assistance at all. The doctors I saw (which by now included an XLH-knowledgeable nephrologist) tried the usual pharmaceutical treatments to lower the PTH levels. However, they not only didn't help but immediately after trying a newer expensive treatment to bring the level down, my creatinine clearance declined further, for the first time since probably childhood. I probably should have been taken off that medication and had surgery then, but instead they just continued making adjustments to the various meds. Eventually I had a subtotal parathyroidectomy. My bone pain disappeared almost entirely; creatinine clearance, however, continues to go lower slowly, and I worry where this will lead.

There still is much difficulty finding doctors who've heard of XLH, let alone have the knowledge to treat it properly, but much progress is being made in the treatment of the condition. I'm excited that it sounds like soon there will be a truly effective treatment available. It will undoubtedly be expensive, but hopefully insurance companies will cover the cost and enable children to grow up with strong, straight bones without the

health consequences of past treatments. That would be
truly wonderful.

# Music Inspires
# by Valery Didula

When I was a one-and-a-half-year-old boy, I had deformities of leg. The doctors said that I had rickets, and I was not treated. At the age of twelve, I was diagnosed with hypophosphatemic rickets and doctors did surgery on my feet in the city, Kurgan.

From this age I have an active lifestyle. I go in for sports: swimming, table tennis, bicycle, gymnastics daily.

I'm a positive man and, of course, music, which for me is the favorite activity and also a job. The first guitar gave me my mother, as I was five years old. Since then I am always with my guitar. I'm a guitarist, writing music in the style of folk-rock music, fusion. Music inspires me and gives strength to people around.

Every year I go with my concerts in Russia and other countries. In 2015, I fulfilled my dream, because we had a crazy concert with the Symphony Orchestra under the direction of the talented Lee Ott.

My mum is seventy-nine years old, and she also has deformities of her legs. She is now walking on crutches. She tries to have an active lifestyle, doing gymnastics and a very positive person.

I have a daughter, who is two-and-a-half-years old. At the age of three months, the doctors diagnosed XLH. She is treated with phosphate supplement.

We consider ourselves to be a happy family.

# Just a Bit Smaller
# by Jessica G.

I'm a second-generation XLHer. I just gave birth to my first child in June and learned at his three-month check-up that he has XLH. I knew it was a 50/50 chance but I was still devastated. I called my mother who also has XLH and she reassured me that his future is not our past, that he has newer treatment options that weren't available thirty-plus years ago. I feel confident that his treatment is going well and that he has a bright future ahead of him. My own childhood, teen, and adult life has been shaped daily by XLH both in positive and negative ways.

As the youngest of three children I worshiped the ground my brother and sister walked on. My brother also has XLH while my sister doesn't. We played, rode bikes, fished, and swam like everyone else. I played softball competitively until high school when I was cut from the junior varsity team. But I didn't give up. I tried out for the lacrosse team as a goalie and made the team. My junior year I was made team captain on the varsity squad and started every game. I went on to play four years of Division III college lacrosse. I was taunted for my size by opposing fans but just ignored it. Were there tears? Of course, but not until I was on the bus or at home. I held my head high and kept my chin up... all 4'9" of me! I went on to become a physical education teacher and coach. I'm teaching the next generation that size doesn't matter. I stay active by mountain biking, snowboarding, and walking, and I play the oboe.

Matthew, my mother, and I would take our quarterly trip to the hospital in Buffalo to see Dr. Margret MacGillivary who was the loveliest, kindest woman I have ever met. Even as a child I knew I was different from everyone else, and when it came time for her to show me where I was on the growth chart I would cry. She would hug and comfort me each and every visit. Wanda was our nurse who always drew my blood even though I was a "tricky stick." I hated getting my blood drawn but became accustomed to the necessary evil. I know I'm going to go through the same process with my son.

As a woman, mother, and teacher living with XLH, I try to show others that even though I may look different, I am still a kind and compassionate person. I smile at those who look at me when I'm out with my husband and son because the majority of the time I get a smile back. I'm as normal as anyone else, just a bit smaller.

# Bicycling Through Life with XLH/VDRR
## by Mary Hawley

Would you believe at four years old when I started kindergarten, I was too short to step up on the first step of the bus? The bus driver had to put the bus in park, get off the bus and lift me up on the first step. I could jump off the step on the way out. This was our morning routine my first year of school. To give you an indication of my size, I was wearing a 4T (Toddler).

My size didn't prevent me from doing much. I grabbed an old neighborhood junk bike with rotted out hard tires that was ten sizes too big for me, and actually made it go. My grandparents saw my sheer tenacity and determination and decided to buy me a little girl's bicycle that summer. Grandpa had to modify the seat to make it go down even further. He also put wooden blocks on the pedals.

Bicycling became my favorite thing to do. I think because it was less painful than to run to keep up with the other kids. On my bike I was free and nobody could tell that I waddled when I walked and couldn't run very well. I could really get around on a bike. I covered a lot of ground—going to the beach, to the river banks, and to the Dairy Queen for an icecream cone. I still haven't given up the habit for over fifty-some years now. I put on 1400 miles this summer, like I do every summer. I rode on the first Bike-Ride-Across-Wisconsin back in

1978 from La Crosse to Milwaukee in five days, on a girl's Schwinn Ten Speed. Today I still ride a 24" girl's mountain bike, which is made for the size of your average eight-year-old.

I was diagnosed in 1963 when times and terminology were different. My parents took me to the doctor because I was profoundly short and bow-legged. When they first saw me they told them they didn't know if I had the treatable (rachitic) or untreatable (achon) form of dwarfism. Blood tests determined I had low phosphorus, so I was treatable, and we learned I had something called Vitamin D Resistant Rickets. I was put on massive dosages of vitamin D, 50,000 I.U. a day. The doctors explained that phosphorus was leaking from my kidneys, like a hole-in-the-bucket, and they were attempting to fill it by giving me massive dosages of Vitamin D. This would require monthly blood tests, and several times my levels were toxic, and I had to immediately stop taking it, along with no milk, cottage cheese or any dairy products, until the levels went down again.

Back then, only the severest cases of XLH/VDRR ever went to the doctor and orthopedic surgeons treated them, as they usually had to do surgery to correct bowlegs along the way. This condition ran in our family for a few generations with my Grandma having a distinctive waddle to her gait. I also had other relatives who were short and bow-legged, but it was always associated with living thru the Great Depression and WWII era. I had a noticeably severe case that could not be explained away by these historic social events of the past.

One thing that I have always remembered was that it wasn't considered a terrible disease back then. In fact, we were told to consider ourselves fortunate, as things could be worse, and I could have had the untreatable type of dwarfism and been a lot shorter. One of the things I distinctly remember are the doctors saying: "She'll be short, stocky and healthy and just have bow-legs and bad teeth."

As a child I was very active and took to riding a bike and I think it was less stressful on the joints than running and walking. Here I am fifty-some years later still riding my bike and in fairly good health. I always attribute that to the doctors of that time, not portraying XLH/VDRR as a terrible disease. "Mind over Matter" type of thing. We simply didn't know any better.

My growth plates closed at twelve years old, and I only attained a height of 4' 3", far short of our goal of 4' 10" that we were striving for all this time. So then, at that time I had femur osteotomies and gained another four inches in height. I always have considered myself very fortunate. Just like when I was younger, nothing every stopped me from doing anything. I married, had three healthy kids, although one has XLH/VDRR. Along with bicycling I go camping, hiking and kayaking. I have traveled internationally to China, Europe and Mexico. I lived in the high Arctic in Alaska for almost a decade and earned an engineering degree from University of Alaska- Fairbanks. I am still very active today, and follow the mantra of "keep moving."

If anything, I'd like to inspire others to follow your dreams, wherever they may take you!

# The Benefits of Exercise
# by Michael Lamoureux

I had a twin brother. We appeared to be identical, but we were actually fraternal. We were born eight weeks premature at Toronto Sick Children's Hospital. We weren't diagnosed with XLH until we were weight bearing age, at which point the bowing in our legs became visible.

Growing up, we were heavily involved in the Canadian Cadet organization, which required prolonged periods of standing. My brother used to carry a heavy drum, while I carried a fifteen-pound rifle. As kids, we didn't understand the potential damage these weight-bearing activities could cause to our bones.

We were on a strict regimen of phosphate and vitamin D to mitigate the effects of XLH, but eventually it became necessary for surgical intervention as we approached our adulthood. Over the course of a decade we had surgical nails bolted in place within each of our tibiae and femurs, depending on the specific need at the time.

When I was in university, I recall having tremendous pain in my tibiae going up and down stairs or even stepping off street curbs walking to my next class. The surgical reinforcement of my leg bones was life-changing for me. For my brother, however, it was far less effective, since the bowing in his legs was more significant than mine. I was able to get up and walk on the same day of the operation, and felt immediate relief from the pain caused by pseudo-fractures that had developed over the years.

With my renewed sense of strength and function, I endeavored to become more athletic. A decade later, I discovered cross training. The cross training movement provided me with a mechanism to systematically test the boundaries of my abilities, and empowered me to reshape those boundaries through short burst of high intensity exercises, including weight-bearing and Olympic-style lifts.

It seems counter-intuitive that I could benefit from weight-bearing workouts, since the weight of my own body had caused the bow in my legs and pseudo-fractures to develop in the first place. What I've come to realize is that these short bursts of high intensity training actually help my bones to endure the constant force of gravity exerted on my body. It's almost as if I'm raising the bar for my bones to adapt, making the load of everyday life that much easier to endure. I can't say for sure whether or not this would still be the case if my bones weren't surgically reinforced.

The most important thing I would emphasize with anyone growing up with XLH is to avoid prolonged weight-bearing activity—including standing—and try short burst, high intensity training instead. Measure your performance so you can find ways to improve, one workout at a time.

# Milestones
# by Andrew Shortall

Recently, I downloaded a book to my e-reader and started reading it. It's a book I've read many times before, but the first time I read it marked a milestone for me. Not just one in my treatment and XLH history, but also in my life.

The book is called *The Lost Years* and it is a Star Trek novel written by J.M. Dillard. I don't need to go into the plot, but it was actually the first Star Trek novel I had ever read. A certain milestone in my life as a Trekkie! And it was brought to me by a close friend, who at the time was my classmate in school. And it just happened to be during the recovery period from my first osteotomy surgery! Again, quite the milestone, as that surgery started me on the road to having straighter legs.

But it got me thinking about how our lives in general are marked with many such milestones, seminal moments that stay with us forever. My life and treatment journey through XLH have been full of such milestones. Some of the most important ones for me include the following:

I remember being in a hospital for tests. And a piece of music was being used as filler on a TV station in between shows rather than showing adverts. I don't recall the nature or reason for the tests. I just remember thinking it was neat that I had a week off school and got to go into hospital and meet new people and have a different experience. Naturally, I went through a battery of tests including bloods, cultures, urine, X-rays, scans and more. I don't remember the full outcome, but that piece of music has stayed with me ever since. It occasionally pops up here or there, or just randomly arrives in my head, playing on repeat. It was only in the last few years that I found out what it was and got a copy. But, I always found it odd how a piece of music from what should have been a traumatic time of my childhood has served as an inspiration for all these years.

My parents got a referral to an endocrinologist who was a specialist in XLH, or Renal Rickets as it was called back then. It might have been soon after the tests, or at least within eighteen months of those tests, but from then on, my life changed. We started to learn more about the condition, thanks to him. I ended up on the right medications: vitamin D and phosphates. And within about two years, my growth, although still stunted, was matching the average growth curve of "normal" children my age.

It was thanks to my new endocrinologist that we were then referred to the surgeon who ultimately performed my osteotomy surgeries. Meeting him was a truly seminal moment as he felt confident that I would after the course of surgeries end up with much straighter legs and an end to having my feet pointing inwards. To this day, my legs are straighter and my feet now point outwards!

As my surgeries came to an end, my endocrinologist then suggested I begin a course of human growth hormone supplements. He wasn't sure it would boost my height by much but he felt it would certainly benefit me. In fact, his words were something along the lines of "it won't do you any harm at all," so we agreed. So then for the next year, I took HGH.

For as long as I can remember, I've been interested in cars. As a young boy, I dreamed of driving a car myself. When I discovered motorsport, I dreamed of driving a racing car. My only barrier at that age was my height. I couldn't reach the pedals. Every few months I'd get in the driver seat of my dad's car, pull the seat forward as much as possible and try to press the clutch. I think somewhere around the age of fifteen, I was finally able to fully press the clutch. For me, this was huge! It meant that someday I'd be able to drive a car. Hopefully. And yes, I finally did learn to drive, pass my test and get my license. I haven't stopped driving since. I've even driven a single-seat racing car, albeit not professionally!

By the time I was seventeen, my growth spurt was about done. I was still on the HGH but it had been a while since we had seen my endocrinologist. My blood levels were stable, and I was working hard in school. It must have been about four months since the last visit, but we went along and as always, I had given bloods for testing. And as always, the nurse took my measurements of weight and height and noted them on my chart. An hour later, my name was called and there was my endocrinologist, beaming a smile at me and my mom. I had no idea what was up, so I just assumed he got some good news. As it turned out, the good news was for me. My levels were still stable, and my weight was good. Something to do with playing street soccer with my neighbors and with my pals in school, too. But, it wasn't that news that made him smile. Seemingly, my height had advanced a tad. I was now, at that stage, 1m 56cm tall, or roughly 5'1," and I'll never forget that he got up from his desk, tightened his bow tie, came around and shook my hand firmly for a good thirty seconds. His sense of pride for my new-found height left me feeling giddy! Yet another true milestone and one that will stay with me as long as I live.

The final milestone was when my treatment ended. The general consensus then was that on reaching an adult age, say eighteen to twenty-one, treatment was no longer necessary. I was effectively discharged from the clinic. Nowadays, I know and believe that I should still be taking some form of medication. It might have prevented the natural deterioration that I'm currently experiencing. Perhaps this moment is bittersweet. I know where it has led me, but at the time I felt great relief at no longer having to swallow pills or take vile-tasting effervescent phosphate tablets in water. It felt like I was free.

There are many other moments in my life that warrant being noted as milestones or even just simply great memories. There are indeed other moments that mark changes in my body and indicated the potential for future troubles. Perhaps these are the times when the trademark determination and almost fiery independence we XLHers are known for isn't necessarily a good thing. And again, there are a few other moments I'd gladly forget or even wish had never happened. But in terms of my life and my XLH journey, these are my milestones. I choose to draw strength from them because they all came together to help make me who I am today.

# The Glass is Half Full, Part Two
## by Nancy J. Alauzen

Two of the less visible effect of XLH are dental abnormalities and hearing loss. I fit the textbook case, having had twenty crowns, multiple root canals, two fixed bridges and several implants and extractions. I proactively have more frequent cleanings than the normally suggested six-month intervals to stay ahead of additional dental complications. Some well-meaning people have suggested it would be more financially prudent to have all my teeth extracted and invest in dentures. For me this isn't an option now. Maybe in the future it might be, but for now I will continue to preserve my teeth and keep my smile!

And I clearly remember the day the audiologist grimly informed me that I needed my first hearing aid. I knew I was in trouble when the hearing test began and there were long periods of silence that I knew should have been filled with audible sounds. The young audiologist delivered the news and I began to cry. I wish I could recall her telling me everything would be fine but instead she stared blankly at me as I tried to comprehend the news. I have since added a hearing aid for the second ear and while I struggle as the audiologist sees a decline in my annual hearing tests, I make sure I wear the aids daily and keep the batteries fresh and the aids clean. I know many individuals put their aids in a drawer for safe keeping but I know that will never help my situation! I do read lips and purposefully position myself front and center when in a classroom type environment. As the hearing loss progresses, I am in the process of making sure I have explored all possible treatment options.

About eight years ago my endocrinologist realized that efforts to regulate tertiary hyperparathyroidism were unsuccessful. A final medication was prescribed in hopes that surgery could be prevented. After trying this medication, it did not produce the needed results and surgery was necessary. This presented a short-term dilemma as my degenerative joint disease required two immediate back-to-back knee replacements. I explained to the endocrinologist that I understood the urgency of the surgery, but without the immediate knee replacements my ability to walk was extremely compromised. After having and successfully healing from both knee replacements, the parathyroid surgery was completed and that is now a closed chapter in my book.

My journey with XLH has presented ongoing and new challenges every year. Two years ago I went for what I thought was a routine follow up with my orthopedic surgeon. During the visit they discovered my body was rejecting my second knee replacement and a third knee replacement was scheduled and completed.

I have realized that XLH is so much more than perfectly straight legs, but approaching XLH with the "glass half full" attitude has made dealing with XLH manageable and not a burden. I am ready for any future challenges that my XLH may present!

# A Perspective on Life
# by Jon Rann

I am an XLH male from the USA and sixty years old. I am five feet tall, and after decades of root canals, the few real teeth remaining in my head support permanent bridgework.

I was diagnosed at two years of age, back when XLH was known as Vitamin D Resistant Rickets. I was prescribed 50,000 units of Vitamin D daily for a decade. Miraculously, I have no kidney or liver problems resulting from this. My mother passed along her XLH to me. She was advised in the 1950s that since no one else in her family had XLH, then her condition couldn't possibly be genetic, and thus could not be passed to her offspring. She was very sad when she learned she had been so ill-advised.

I made the decision long ago (probably during one of my many lengthy stays in various hospitals in the mid-1960s when I was eleven or so) to never father any children of my own. My disease will go to the grave with me.

I have one sister, four years younger than I, who does not have XLH. My parents dragged her along with us on every visit to the hospitals. XLH affects everyone within a family, not just the victims of the disease. Although neither of my parents would ever admit it, I strongly suspect that their having to cope with my illness (and they were both always there for me) was a contributing, stressful factor in their eventual divorce.

For the record, I do not blame my parents for my condition, and I do not curse my fate. I am neither bitter, nor do I define myself as a victim of XLH, any more than I am a victim of having brown eyes. I was raised to understand that everyone is different and everyone deals with their own problems in their own way, as best they can.

I was the only child with XLH in the hospital. When I first arrived, I was surrounded by curious children in the orthopedic ward, who asked me, "Why are you here...?" I thought my bowed legs might have suggested a self-evident explanation, but then one nearby child in a wheelchair added, "...when you can walk?" That one remark put the rest of my life into perspective for me. Most of the children in my ward would never walk as well as I did, if at all. Many had far more severe birth defects. Several were mentally retarded, as well. As frightening as these charity hospitals were in the 1960s, they were even worse for my mother in the 1930s.

Aside from the three major osteotomies I had (the most painful and profound being performed on my right femur), I managed to break my left femur in the same place three times during my lifetime—in elementary school, high school, and in college. I still have nightmares, not about the pain of these fractures, but about the sound my breaking femur made—like a wet tree limb snapping. After the last fracture, I had my left femur reinforced with stainless steel, as my right femur had been years earlier. Best decision I ever made! I have been taking calcitriol daily for the past decade or so, as per my endocrinologist.

The childhood osteotomy on my lower left leg was not as well done as the others. When I was about thirty years old it started causing me increasing distress and discomfort, to the point where I had to walk with a cane, even around my own home, by the time I was forty. I opted for another osteotomy, which turned out even worse than the previous one, and took much longer to heal than the surgeon forecast. My legs hurt all the time now, especially when I walk. Opiate therapy for my "ambient" bone pain and my acute, "breakthrough" pain keeps me active and independent. Without opiates to manage my chronic pain I would have little quality of life, and would sleep very poorly.

# Did You Know?
# by Gin Jones

"Did you know?" a friend asked me a few years ago. "Did you know you'd end up like this?"

He didn't have to explain what he meant by "like this." It referred to the stooped spine, restricted range of motion in all of my joints, and the kind of difficulty with walking that would have been more typical of a person in her eighties, rather than my actual age of fifty-seven.

We were at our thirty-fifth college reunion, and it was a school known for the wide range of outdoor sports available to students and for its support of physical fitness. I'd always been terrible at most sports, but throughout college I was on the swim team and I ran up to my sixth-floor dorm room several times a day without any noticeable effort. While most of my classmates at the reunion looked like they'd soon be proving that sixty is the new forty, I was old and decrepit before my time.

I'd lived through the gradual changes and didn't notice them much on a daily basis, but my friend hadn't seen me in ten years. He was clearly shocked by the changes he saw, and couldn't reconcile them with the person he'd gone to school with. I completely understood why he asked, "Did you know?"

I brushed it off, making light of my challenges, but later I kept coming back to the question after the reunion was over.

The superficial answer was easy: No, I didn't know. I'm one of many, many, many XLHers who, once the growth plates closed, were essentially told that we were done with the XLH experience. It took another fifteen years before I started to realize that wasn't true. And probably ten more years before my suspicion that my joint problems were related to XLH was confirmed by my reading of the medical literature, although even then, they were barely mentioned. That's the thing about having a rare disease, exacerbated by being, as I am, a spontaneous case, so I don't have any relatives with the condition. I'd never met anyone with XLH until I was in my fifties, and I'd never seen what it could do to spines and joints and ligaments.

The deeper question was harder to answer: would the experience have been better if I'd known what to expect as I aged with my XLH?

I don't have a good answer for that. There are several ways in which having that warning would have been useful. It might have motivated me to lose weight and engage in regular physical exercise. A healthy weight and daily exercise is good for everyone, but it's particularly important for anyone with compromised bone structure. I'll never know for sure, but I might have slowed down the progression of my arthritis and calcifications if I'd been lighter and more active.

Knowing that I'd have increasing daily pain and mobility restrictions might have helped me to appreciate the things I could do before I lost those abilities. It might also have inspired me to be kinder to myself on days when pain and chronic fatigue kept me from accomplishing everything I wanted to do. There were many times when I called myself lazy, when the reality was that I was physically unable to do things. With some warning of what was to come, I might have been more prepared, and I could have worked on a state of acceptance, instead of being so angry about what felt like an ambush by the pain, fatigue, and mobility restrictions.

On the other hand, I have to wonder if knowing what was to come might have had some negative consequences. Believing I could do anything (except run or do things that required being over five feet tall) gave me the freedom to go to college and law school, practice law, and pursue a normal life. I never questioned whether I'd have the necessary stamina and physical abilities to grow a huge organic garden, make quilts, or serve as the general contractor (and painter) for a huge addition to my house. If I'd known that my skeleton and muscles continued to be compromised by the lack of phosphorus, would I have been that fearless? Would I have been more inclined to go easy on myself when it came to setting goals? Would I have been even more inclined to be lazy, since I had a legitimate excuse of being chronically ill?

I'll never know for sure whether my life would have been different if I'd known back in college what my physical condition would be forty years later. I'd like to think that the knowledge would have helped me to accomplish more of my goals. I'm not sure much would have changed, though. There are days now when I can't do everything I want to because of my messed-up bones and endocrine system, but if I care about something enough, like writing books, making quilts and advocating for fellow XLHers, I'll find a way to do it.

# Height Doesn't Matter
## by Marina Velazquez

I was born in Madrid, Spain, moved to Puerto Rico, and eventually moved to the United States. It was when I was getting my Chemical Engineering degree that I developed a passion for computers. Then I finished a Masters in Engineering Management. My academic skills have taken me around the world. I visited Mexico, Venezuela, Brazil, Spain, France, England, Italy, Greece, the Netherlands, China, Korea and Japan on business trips. I love that in Japan I can sit in any chair and still be able to reach the floor without my feet hanging in the air! My boss hates it. But he is 6'4" and I am 4'6".

Working in a business dominated by tall men has given me many interesting opportunities to show that different is good. I work long-distance a lot, talking to customers and peers over the phone. And I often get a laugh when some of them met me face to face. I can see the surprised expression on their face when they see someone so short. The first thing that came out of the mouth of one man was, "Where is the rest of you? No offense, but really, I was expecting a six-foot-tall woman; you speak over the phone with such confidence level that I would never have thought that you were so short. I apologize for my small brain."

I often give presentations. A year ago, they were planning to have the panelists sit on high, bar-stool type chairs for some casual chat on stage. When the organizer mentioned that during a planning phone conference, I said, "I don't think so." All other participants on the call started laughing. One of them clarified to the organizer, "You'll understand when you met Marina. Just bring regular chairs."

When I speak to an audience, I like to take the microphone and move out from behind the podium and say, "You came to see me, not just to hear me." That melts the ice and people pay more attention to my presentation.

Besides work, I am a wife and a mother. At home, I made some modifications. I have a "his and hers" kitchen. I have a stove-top on cabinets that reach my belly, the height of my husband's pants inseam. The cabinets with the sink and the dishwasher, which are at a normal level height, reach my upper torso. On my side, I cook; on his side ("Honey, I cannot reach to do the dishes, would you do them?"), he cleans.

My kids have learned that the size of a person is not measured in feet and inches, and that you can be all you set yourself to be. XLH or not, short or tall, one should always live life at its fullest and have fun on the way.

In my spare time, I am a Catholic Religious Educator, and it is a joy discussing God with teenagers. All my students are taller than me, and when I see them the first few days, they do not know what to think of me. I remember one time walking in a parking lot in town and a group of teens looked at me and some started laughing and making comments about me. One of my students stood up to say, "You guys, respect, that's my teacher."

# Aging With XLH
# by Lorna Brandt

After treatment and surgeries in my childhood, I maintained periodic contact with doctors, having the recommended lab work done. In later years, in my late forties and early fifties, I began having more problems with pain due to arthritis in the knee joints as well as stress fractures, and I started using a cane again. I was in touch with a local orthopedist and had injections in my knees to alleviate some of the pain in an attempt to hold off knee replacement surgery for a few years. My orthopedist later recommended that I have the surgery done at a teaching institution due to the more complex diagnosis.

The choice I made was to return to the other clinic where I had not been seen since a young child, primarily for another opinion on the medication regimen. This choice was made after some study on The XLH Network, Inc. website, which I had discovered after getting my first personal computer in 2000. This was an excellent resource for me to learn about XLH and other related issues. For the last several years, I have been on calcitriol and a calcium/magnesium/vitamin-D supplement. At one time, I did take phosphorus supplements, and later had issues with hypercalcemia for which I had two parathyroid surgeries.

I had my first knee replacement just before my fifty-ninth birthday, and it was like a miracle. Replacement of the other knee took place two and a half years later. In both cases, I was bone on bone in the knee joint area, but have done very well for over ten years with the new knees.

Regarding dental issues, my mother told me on several occasions that when I was a young child, many people would comment on how beautiful my teeth were. I'm not sure when I started having abscesses, but it was either in the teens or as a young adult. Repeated abscesses below the lower front teeth resulted in the dentist pulling the four front lower teeth and putting in a bridge. I never had problems in that area after that. As years went by, I had several more abscesses here and there, one tooth at a time, followed by a root canal and then placement of a cap on the tooth.

Over the years I have sometimes been referred to as a dwarf, and I try to explain that there is a difference. After carefully explaining what I knew of XLH to a younger person of college age that I knew well, she just would not believe me, and insisted I was a dwarf. Something like that can be pretty frustrating, but again I just had to realize that I tried my best and it didn't work, so I needed to try to forget it.

I've also had many great friends who included me in their lives, and my close family members have always treated me like everyone else, whether being helpful in some way or even being part of a fun joke. My twin sister and I each had our own friends as well as some friends in common, and we were often involved in some of the same activities as well as some different activities at home, in school and at church. We both did babysitting for our first paid jobs. At slumber parties or other get-togethers with friends, many of the other girls sat on the floor with their knees toward the outside of their body and their lower legs bent to the inside with feet crossed. Much as I tried, I could never do that. However, I could do the opposite, with my knees bent toward the inside and touching each other, and the feet going to the outside. The other girls were so amazed that I could do that, and they would try to do the same thing but couldn't.

The main thing in life that I wish could have turned out differently would be to have had a husband, children, and grandchildren with whom to share life. But I was fortunate at times to be around nieces and nephews and children of friends as they were growing up, and I was able to help care for them and do special things with them, helping them to learn and grow.

As I have grown older, I feel somewhat taller in comparison to some friends and family. Some seem to be shrinking a little bit as part of the normal aging process, whereas I have actually gained a bit in height following the knee replacements. Of course we can all chuckle about that. I do have problems reaching things on high shelves in the stores, and there is usually help available either from store employees or from other shoppers. This also reminds me to assist others as I can, such as those in wheelchairs or using a walker or a riding cart from the store.

# What You Mourn
# by Sheila Black

The year they straightened my legs,
the young doctor said, meaning to be kind,
Now you will walk straight
on your wedding day, but what he could not
imagine is how even on my wedding day
I would arch back and wonder
about that body I had before I was changed,
how I would have nested in it
made it my home, how I repeated his words,
when I wished to stir up my native anger,
feel like the exile I believed
I was, imprisoned in a foreign body
like a person imprisoned in a foreign land,
forced to speak a strange tongue,
heavy in the mouth, a mouth full of stones.

Crippled they called us when I was young,
later the word was *disabled* and then *differently abled*,
but those were all names given by outsiders,
none of whom could imagine
that the crooked body they spoke of,
the body, which made walking difficult
and running impossible,
except as a kind of dance, a sideways looping
like someone about to fall
headlong down and hug the earth, that body

they tried so hard to fix, straighten was simply mine,
and I loved it as you love your own country,
the familiar lay of the land, the unkempt trees,
the smell of mowed grass, down to the nameless
flowers at your feet--clover, asphodel,
and the blue flies that buzz over them.

# XLH DAY

## Love, Support, and Community
## by Elizabeth Olear

Just a short time ago, in April 2011, XLH Day did not yet exist. At least, it did not yet exist as a gathering of patients and families, clinical and research experts in the field of metabolic bone disease, and it certainly did not exist as an annual event known by a community of patients around the world.

In April 2011, XLH Day was still just an idea for patients to meet other patients, for clinicians and researchers to meet more than just a single patient here and there, and for people from Connecticut to California, Canada to Alaska to meet someone else outside their family who was "just like them."

It was the question, "Do you know anyone else who is just like me," that inspired the idea for a patient and family day. In April 2011, I had been working with Dr. Thomas Carpenter at the Yale Center for XLH for just a little over five years, and from the beginning of my time working at Yale, I had met and seen children and adults with XLH on a weekly, if not daily basis. And I was asked the question, "Do you know anyone else…" on a weekly, if not daily basis. One day after telling a surprised patient that she was my fifth patient with XLH that I had already seen that week (and it was only Tuesday!), I started to consider that although it was great for Dr. Carpenter and me to know so many patients with XLH, it would be even better for them to know each other.

My wheels started turning as I tried to figure out how to make this "XLH Patient and Family Day" a reality, and I began to run this idea by a few of the patients and families who might be interested in such an event. Fortunately, I did not have to look very far to find Arlene Iorizzo and her wonderful family. Arlene opened her heart and her home to the idea of XLH Day and recruited her family, her husband, Greg, and children, Jason and Gina, along with her siblings, most notably, Bill and Liz Coogan and many of her friends and neighbors to make this very important day in XLH history a reality.

The very first XLH Day took place at The Iorizzo Residence in Hopewell Junction, New York, on September 10, 2011. At the time, I had known the community of patients with XLH for only six short years, but I felt that I was able to know many of our patients' stories (histories), their pains and frustrations, their struggles and disappointments, just from the nature of our interactions over the years. I felt that this day of recognition, a day set aside to acknowledge and celebrate people who live with XLH, and a day with the opportunity to meet others who share the same symptoms, the same struggles, and the same hope was so important for a group of people who may have been misdiagnosed or mismanaged, who may look differently and walk differently than anyone else they know. What a difference it might make for a young child with XLH if they could grow up with a friend who was "just like them" instead of feeling completely different from everyone else.

I stumbled across an email sent to my fellow organizers just after that first event, and my heart is happy:

*If I haven't already told you…how overwhelmed I was on Saturday and how touched I was to see XLH Day finally a reality, please know that this experience of organizing, coordinating and executing XLH Day has been one of the most worthwhile and productive activities in which I've had the honor of participating. I've already seen several patients and their families in clinic and on the research floor this week and they could not stop talking about the events of Saturday—it meant more to our patients and their families than we could have imagined. I do feel sad when I think of my patient who was not allowed to leave the hospital to attend XLH Day—he could not believe there were so many people with XLH in one place and one time and that clinical and research experts took the time to talk to them. Don't worry—we brought him an XLH Day shirt AND we promised to introduce him to the caring group of people who came together to make XLH Day the tremendous success that it was. He told me he has waited 50 years for something like this.*

It was wonderful to hear this and to know that the first XLH Day was received so well. I am pleased that XLH Day has continued since that first gathering in 2011. It has grown and continues to make a tremendous impact on patients with XLH and their families.

In the six years since the first XLH Day, the clinical research community has worked tirelessly to bring a new medication to XLH patients. Recently the European Medicines Agency came to New Haven for an inspection, part of the process to gain approval for the very first drug that targets phosphate wasting in patients with XLH. The possibility of a new treatment for a rare disorder is exciting and with it comes hope for the future of patients with XLH. KRN23/burosumab may be the first commercially available treatment for patients with XLH, but in my heart, I know that the love, support and community that went into the first XLH Day has been some of the best medicine for this patient population.

*Editor's note: Since the first XLH Day in 2011, the event has been held annually in the United States. The first two were in New York, then 2013 and 2017 were in Connecticut, 2014 in Indiana, 2015 in California, and 2016 in Texas. There have also been two XLH Days in England. We look forward to bringing it to different parts of the United States in the future and eventually to other countries as well. You can see pictures from previous events at our official Facebook page: https://www.facebook.com/xlhnetwork/.*

# Comparing Notes at XLH Day
# by Nancy J. Alauzen

My first XLH Day quickly transitioned into a full weekend in September 2011. In order to make the 470-plus-mile trip, I maximized my travel plans to include a follow-up visit to my XLH specialist.

Prior to this event, I only knew one other woman with XLH, and it had taken fifty-plus years to meet Sarah. In the summer of 2010, I sought a second opinion regarding managing my XLH and another resulting condition, tertiary hyperparathyroidism. My new doctor recommended a parathyroidectomy eight weeks later. On this visit, one of the staff introduced Sarah to me, and we became friends. It was amazing to finally meet someone else with the exact diagnosis, as the condition is rare, with an incidence of only one in 20,000 people.

When the announcement of the first XLH Day arrived via email, I called Sarah and we both wanted to attend. We made all the arrangements to share a room and attend the event together. When we arrived at the sprawling home on a cul-de-sac, there was plenty of space for every guest and a large yard to hold all of the festivities. There was also a mini classroom-style layout in the home where the speakers would share their knowledge. I still proudly wear my T-shirt from that first XLH Day.

I spent the entire day meeting and talking with people from Canada, Rhode Island, Maine, New York, North Carolina, and others from Pennsylvania, like myself. Many of the attendees had XLH, but others were unaffected parents of children with the disorder and hoping as I did to learn from the experts and share with others more about our condition. I had so many questions to ask. I wanted to know how and when they were diagnosed, the number of physicians it took to get the proper diagnosis, and more about their successes and challenges along the journey. I was curious to compare notes about the medications they took to manage their XLH.

It was such a fabulous day. I met dozens and dozens of adults and children with XLH. I was taller than a fair number of them. That was unusual. It was also the first time I met men and children with XLH.

There was plenty of delicious food during the entire day, live music, games and activities for the children, mini-massages for the affected adults, and interesting conversation all day long.

Spending the day with the others made me realize that I have a relatively mild case in terms of physical pain. I didn't have as much of the joint and back pain and other symptoms that others had. I have, however, had significant dental abnormalities, and I joke about my fifty-thousand-dollar smile, the amount of money I have paid to address dental issues resulting from the disease.

During the first XLH Day, I sat in several lectures and found them all fascinating. The speakers were all discussing the disease I had lived with for fifty-plus years. I soaked up all the new information, listening intently to every word. I had an opportunity to meet one of the foremost experts on XLH.

When the weekend was over, I felt grateful to have been surrounded by others with XLH. These newfound friends would offer support and friendship in coming years. I felt like I had arrived.

# Late Bloomer
# by Gini Patrick

In 1957, when I was fourteen months old, I was diagnosed with a little-known illness called Vitamin D Resistant Rickets. Fifty years later I stumbled across The XLH Network, Inc. online, and discovered what I *really* had was a metabolic bone disease called X-linked Hypophosphatemia, aka XLH. Imagine my surprise!

You might be thinking to yourself right about now; "How could anyone with this disease know nothing about XLH for all those years?" It does seem a bit odd, I have to admit, but nonetheless, it's true.

I had spent much of the first sixteen years of my life in and out of a hospital for children. So, when I was discharged from the hospital for the last time in 1973, I was more than ready to create a life all my own. Each year my family doctor would order labs and X-rays to make sure all was stable with my health. I never met a doctor who had treated anyone else with my diagnosis. In fact, I grew so accustomed to this scenario, that it never occurred to me how dramatically things might be changing concerning treatments and research for my disease. In short, for fifty years I was telling doctors my story and how to treat me, and they all willingly complied. End of story.....or so I thought.

Finding the Network was like opening a door to another dimension. There were people from all over the country, and in some cases the world, who were comparing notes, asking questions, sharing info about medicines and surgeries, etc. There were links to articles by doctors and research scientists, and discussions on aging with XLH, and all kinds of sources for information I had never known existed. When I received an email announcing the first Midwest XLH Day, I could hardly wait and signed up pronto!

Mom and I were among the first to arrive at the site. As we signed in, I noticed a table with coffee, tea, and snacks on it, so I made a beeline for that destination. Simultaneously, a man who wasn't a guest speaker or board member came right up to me and said: "Hello! My name is____, and you are the first person I've ever met who has XLH too!" As he put out his hand to shake mine we both smiled at each other and started telling our stories. Soon more people arrived and my circle of compatriots in the "Land of XLH" grew quickly right before my eyes. I felt a bit overwhelmed emotionally, but was still able to enjoy the moment as those around me introduced themselves and joined in the conversation. Soon I was surrounded by adults and children of all shapes, sizes, and ages with one thing in common: XLH!

When everyone started filing into the auditorium, I realized that among all of the XLHers around me, I was in fact the tallest one! At five feet tall I am very unfamiliar with that particular feeling. Both my brother and sister were just under six feet tall when they were teen-agers, so even in my own family I was always the smallest of the bunch. I have to admit it was a bit of a rush to notice this situation, but that feeling was quickly followed by thoughts of concern and empathy, for I know all too well what it's like to be the smallest person in the room. I was filled with compassion for all the kids there who were dealing with issues of feeling outcast, or of being bullied by others at schools or in public places. This was the first of many times through-out the day when my eyes were filled with tears. However, I must say it was also the first time in my life that I felt truly in my element around strangers. In fact, I felt that I was *with* my people, my tribe, my commu-nity, and it was a great feeling indeed! I will always treasure that experience of kinship and how comforta-bly it fit….like putting on an old glove that was so worn it had become a second skin.

Over the next few hours there were presentations from guest speakers who were all doctors working with XLH patients in various capacities. I repeatedly felt like I had missed out on a lifetime of information. For example, I had never been to see an endocrinologist for my medical needs. I didn't even know my condition *was* metabolic prior to reading about it on The XLH Network, Inc. website.

After the final Q&A portion of the conference eve-ryone was gathered for a group photo which was later posted on The XLH Network, Inc. Facebook page. I still occasionally go to that page just to take another look at all of us standing there and to reminisce.

When I got back to my own home, I couldn't shake how differently I felt inside. I was more comfortable in my own skin than I had felt since I was old enough to know the difference between able and disabled, normal and abnormal, at ease or diseased. What a wonderful feeling that was, and I still cherish the opportunity I was given to feel it deeply before my days were done.

So, I may be a late bloomer when it comes to XLH and all that goes with it, but that doesn't concern me now, because I have realized my own identity on a level I never knew before, and to use a familiar phrase: It's a good thing.

*Editors' note: This is a much-condensed excerpt from Gini Patrick's memoir,* On the Ward: Tales from a Children's Hospital, *available at major online booksellers.*

# FINAL THOUGHTS

## The Science Fiction

Scientific understanding of XLH is growing exponentially. It took about forty years to get from the initial theory in the 1930s that XLH was caused by resistance to vitamin D to realizing it was actually a phosphate metabolism problem. Then another twenty years passed until the next major step forward, the discovery of Fibroblast Growth Factor 23 (FGF23), which causes the phosphate-wasting.

Now, research offers several potential paths to treatment and a cure. One path is the development of an antibody to FGF23, which, while not a permanent cure, may be able to stop the phosphate-wasting for the duration of treatment. Such an antibody, known as burosumab (formerly KRN23), is currently in clinical trials and under consideration for FDA approval.

Another path involves getting behind the blood levels of FGF23 to the site in the body where it is manufactured, and figuring out why too much is produced. That answer may offer new treatment options or possibly a cure.

And finally there is the long-anticipated prospect of genome editing, once considered more science fiction than science fact. Recent advances, however, suggest that it's just a matter of time before scientists will be able to cure the condition by targeting a defective gene, like the PHEX mutations that cause XLH, and replace it with a working gene.

# What's Normal?
## by Gin Jones

One of the challenges for a patient with a rare disease is not knowing what's "normal." I don't mean compared to the general population—I'll never be normal in that sense—or even compared to one's family—I'd be a foot taller if that were the case—but compared to others within the specific rare disease population.

Many XLH patients have several members in their extended family who also have the condition, so they can see what happens over time. Not all XLHers are that fortunate, though. I'm the only person in my family to have XLH, and none of my doctors had other XLH patients, so I was in my late forties before I met another XLHer online, and then another ten years passed before I met another XLHer in person.

Before I joined the Network, I was completely unaware that there were any adult symptoms of XLH. Like many rare disease patients, I'd been released from treatment when I reached young adulthood with no warning that there might be problems down the road. I developed arthritis and calcifications in my late twenties, but it wasn't until I joined the Network when I was in my forties that I knew those were typical symptoms of adults with XLH. All of a sudden, I learned that so much of what I experienced that was "abnormal" compared to my peers in the general population was "normal" among the XLH community.

One of my first comments on the listserv was to ask about a feeling of hesitation when I stand after I've been off my feet for a while. It's worsened with age, but as far back as when I was in college, I noticed that I couldn't simply start walking again as soon as I stood up at the end of a class. While my classmates were racing out the door for lunch, I was standing next to my seat, waiting for my feet to adapt to bearing my weight. The responses I received from other XLHers confirmed that it wasn't just me, but it was something that a lot of us experience. No one had a solution or even an explanation, but at least I knew I wasn't alone and I wasn't imagining it. For patients who are frequently told that their symptoms are either impossible or imaginary, it's incredibly important to have our experiences validated.

In addition to being validated by the community, I gained the information necessary to know when doctors tried to push me in the wrong direction, which in turn gave me the strength to say no to bad advice. At one point in my forties, I was considering hip replacement surgery and consulted an orthopedic surgeon who claimed to have experience with XLH. He might have seen some pediatric cases, not adults, and he clearly didn't know the limits of his knowledge. He tried to tell me, first, that I didn't have XLH, because my legs "weren't crooked enough." The conversation went downhill from there, as he tried to tell me he knew better than all the doctors who'd relied on blood tests and

X-rays for the diagnosis, and that, in any event, whether I had a metabolic bone disorder was completely irrelevant to the chances of success from orthopedic surgery.

What the doctor didn't know, but that I did, thanks to the Network, was that it is normal for adults with XLH to have extensive calcification of ligaments, like the ones it would turn out I had that were causing the pain in my hips. He didn't know that the phosphate-wasting of XLH can (in some cases, not all) delay bone healing far beyond the "normal" healing period. He didn't know that most of the experts in XLH recommend being on treatment for several months before and after orthopedic surgery.

Fortunately, I did know all of that. I knew the doctor was flat-out wrong in recommending surgery without considering the consequences of my XLH, and I knew that the patient community would support my rejection of the bad advice. I sought a second opinion from someone who acknowledged that a metabolic bone disorder might well affect the bone-healing process, so together we could make the right decision for me.

Ultimately, I opted not to have the hip replacement and more than a dozen years later, I have no regrets about it. I worry, though, about the patients who don't have a community supporting them, who aren't aware of the potential risks specific to XLH, and who might have let an uninformed doctor steamroll them into doing something that wasn't in their best interest.

And that's why I'm so active with the Network, doing my part to bring more patients into our community and to support other patients in learning what's "normal" and what information they need to make the best health care decisions possible.

.

# What Can XLHers do?

XLH patients probably won't be playing professional basketball (until we have a cure or at least an effective treatment), but for anything that doesn't require height, XLHers can and do participate in a wide variety of careers and activities.

It shouldn't surprise anyone to hear that XLHers engage in a number of professional careers, including doctors, lawyers, teachers, nurses, writers, researchers, engineers and assorted computer/tech-related jobs. We also heard from a professional chef, a loan officer, a real estate agent, a mental health therapist and a master florist!

It's a little more surprising, given the physical limitations experienced by many adults with XLH, that quite a few engage in strenuous activities like building rock walls, logging, shooting targets, biking, horseback riding ("even if I can't do all the things on horseback I wish I could, any riding is better than no riding"), drumming ("I've fractured my arms a lot since I started drumming, but it's too much fun to avoid doing"), and even triathlon competition (jointly with her husband; he does the running, and she does the biking and swimming).

Here's a collection of XLHers' descriptions of "what they do," in their own words. We think you'll agree that, ultimately, XLHers can do just about anything they want to do!

**I work as a program analyst** ... and run a mentorship program linking students with alumni. I also used to work a lot in fashion and styling photo shoots and people. Fun stuff. I'm a cyclist and I do long charity rides.

**I volunteer as a USA Swimming Official** at meets hosted by my daughter's swim club and help out from time to time at other clubs and high school meets. I am an avid target shooter and compete at local matches.

**What do I do?** First for no pay: water color artist, run twenty-five miles a week, organic gardening (I eat only a whole food plant based diet). What do I do for pay? I am a real estate agent and an Independent Marketing Director in Direct Sales.

**I work in the logging industry.** Currently I operate my own loader/slasher to prepare and load wood on trucks for logs/pulp/stove wood.

**I have worked as a Registered Nurse for thirty-five years.** I was strongly discouraged by my high school and college counselors from wanting to go into a profession that required me to be on my feet so much. I have always been passionate about nursing and have never regretted a minute of it. I am now fifty-eight years old and may have to retire early as I am getting more tired and having more pain, but I am so thankful I was able to fulfill my lifelong dream. My other passion is music and I have recorded a CD of my singing and had so much fun doing it. I am blessed!

**I am a Radiologic Technologist (X-ray tech)/ Mammographer**. I love what I do! It is very rewarding to be a part of helping women with breast diseases. Sometimes it's just listening to the amazing stories of what these courageous women and sometimes men have been through. I was a Registered Dental Assistant first. I think because of all my teeth problems I was drawn to learning more about dentistry. Being in that field guided me into what I really love, which is taking x-rays. It is seriously my calling in life. It is sometimes a daily struggle to work and be on my feet so much. I use ice packs on my back and knees frequently because of the pain and swelling that I experience.

**I am a professional piano technician** and have been for over twenty-five years. I tune and repair pianos and some other stringed instruments. I am also a musician (guitar, banjo, hammered dulcimer and ukulele, primarily) and occasionally teach private lessons on those instruments. That's what I do for a living. For fun, I do other things like woodworking, reading, knitting, writing and photography.

**I am a visual artist** who successfully supported myself with my creative skills for almost fifteen out of the forty years I worked. I focused primarily on assemblage, found object, and collage, but also did detail painting for other artisans, and design work for various entrepreneurs. During the times when I wasn't able to support myself through my artwork I held a variety of jobs in order to support my art "habit." I've been a waitress, a short order cook, a woodworker, a retail store manager, and a custodian, to name a few. My last paying job was as a lab courier for a local hospital, but I had to eventually give that up due to mobility/pain issues with my XLH.

**I used to work in Accounts Payable** for over twenty years, but I am no longer able to work due to mobility and pain issues. I do miss working and getting out and seeing people every day, not to mention making money! My real passion though is counted cross stitch! It relaxes me and takes my mind off things like pain and swelling.

**I am a board certified ob/gyn**. I also crochet and run occasionally. International medicine is one of my hobbies, and I have been to both Europe and Asia on medical trips.

**I'm a registered nurse**. I do that for pay, of course. ;) Other than that, I'm more of a homebody who prefers to keep to myself. I guess that's because I'm very introverted, but I also blame the XLH for me not wanting to really be "out there" or draw attention to myself.

**Travel is probably my first love**, but I'm very passionate about cars, love car races, shows, etc. Photography is another hobby of mine as well as reading.

**I enjoy travel, photography, cooking, sewing, English Country Dancing** (think Jane Austen), and historic re-enacting (Lewis & Clark era). XLH has interfered with the English Country Dancing, and now the livelier dances bother my knees, but our family started hosting an annual dance series for about 150 area homeschoolers about ten years ago, so I became more of a facilitator. Our two kids became pretty good at organizing and calling dances themselves, as well as lively dancers! The XLH slowed me down a bit as a re-enactor, as I could only walk and stand so much, but fortunately there were plenty of benches around that I could use to sit and hand-sew, and still interact with the tourists! Budget cuts killed the program, but my knees were just as glad!

**I coach creative entrepreneurs** and write books in the self-help and creativity genre, including having published 2 bestsellers. My background in my young twenties was professional musical theatre. I left for multiple reasons, one of them being physical limitations with XLH, although I wouldn't go as far as saying that it was XLH alone caused me to cease doing it. I've recently started directing children's theatre again for fun, which has been great.

**I was interested in the medical field, but knew that I would not have the stamina** to work as a doctor or nurse, so I pursued the field of Medical Records Administration. I worked in that field for over thirty-five years. I also taught medical terminology, coding, and transcription for a couple years at a local community college. I have enjoyed working, and take pride in owning my own home, and taking care of things including cleaning, painting, mowing and gardening for many of those years. Of course the aging process is slowing me down a bit, but I can't do much about that. Other activities I have enjoyed over the years include singing in church choir, and participation in various other church activities, genealogy organizations, etc., and have enjoyed my pet dogs, plus sewing, embroidery, knitting, baking, canning, and cake decorating.

# ABOUT THE NETWORK

The XLH Network, Inc., began as a global website and listserv in 1996, thanks to the hard work of Larry Winger (England), Colin Steeksma (Canada) and Joely Macheel (United States). As the community grew, volunteers maintained the educational website, created a flyer with basic information about XLH, and attended medical conferences to spread awareness of XLH.

Larry Winger and Joan Reed presented what may have been the first patient-organization-written poster at the annual conference of the American Society for Bone and Mineralization Research (ASBMR). It was entitled "Self-actualized Perceptions of X-Linked Hypophosphatemia Suggest a Pro-active role for Patient-Support Networks in Managing Patients with this Rare Metabolic Bone Disorder," and you can see it here: www.xlhnetwork.org/weak-bones-strong-wills. Larry Winger also published an article, "Living With Genetic Rickets" in *Archives of Disease in Childhood*, a leading peer-reviewed pediatrics journal. You can read it here: http://www.ncbi.nlm.nih.gov/pmc/articles/PMC1719886/pdf/v089p00390.pdf.

Also during those early years (although we can't take credit for it!), genetic testing for XLH became commercially available, Fibroblast Growth Factor 23 (FGF23) was discovered, and research began for developing an antibody to FGF23.

In 2005, when the listerv had reached about 500 members (including patients, family and health-care providers), the Network was incorporated as a 501(c)(3) nonprofit in the United States. The first officers were Joan Reed, President; Joanne Joseph, Vice-President; Kathy Buchanan, Secretary; and Denise Lentz, Treasurer.

The mission of The XLH Network, Inc. is to promote XLH awareness and education for affected families, medical professionals, and the community at-large; to support physicians and other providers of medical care for better diagnosis and treatment; to create resources and a community for affected individuals and their families so they can understand and cope with the complications of the disease; and to foster the search for a cure.

Since incorporating, the Network has continued to maintain an educational website and a discussion platform, distribute flyers with basic information about XLH (including one that provides a general overview, another that focuses on dental issues and most recently, age-appropriate information for children with XLH), and attend medical events like the conferences of AS-BMR and the Endocrine Society. Plans are underway to expand to additional conferences, such as those held by pediatricians, nurse-practitioners, and dentists. The

Network also organizes an annual patient-focused, educational and networking event, called XLH Day.

The most ambitious project to date is the design, construction and launch (in late 2017) of the first ever Natural History Study and Patient Registry for XLH (and the related phosphate-wasting disorders): https://xlhnaturalhistory.iamrare.org/.

The Network's Registry and Data are part of the National Organization for Rare Disorders' (NORD) Natural History Program. We are thankful for NORD's investment in the health and wellbeing of all rare disorder communities, including ours.

The Network has been fortunate to have the support and advice of a stellar Scientific Advisory Board. They have guided us over the years, although of course any errors we may have made are entirely our own. The current members are:

Carolyn D. Macica, Ph.D., Chair

Thomas O. Carpenter, M.D.

Michael Econs, M.D.

Suzanne Jan de Beur, M.D.

Peter S.N. Rowe, Ph.D.

Raghbir Kaur, D.M.D.

Maya Helene Doyle, Ph.D., LCSW-R

# ABOUT THE XLH NATURAL HISTORY STUDY AND REGISTRY

In 2017, The XLH Network, Inc. launched the largest-ever study to research diseases associated with genetic and tumor-induced hypophosphatemia, diseases that currently have no cure. In some ways, the XLH Natural History Study and Registry will provide insights into stories of XLH in the same ways *Weak Bones, Strong Wills* tells the stories of our members. But instead of narratives, the study will help researchers put together the bits and pieces of our stories by combining them into searchable data. New patterns, questions, and answers can emerge when all of our stories are combined.

The natural history study will provide a complete picture of each patient's experience with XLH, and the initiative will help fill the missing link researchers and medical experts need to discover new therapies for hypophosphatemia and other potentially related disorders, and like this book, it is dependent on community members "telling" their stories.

The XLH Natural History Study and Registry is a natural history study that consists of electronic surveys to collect information about the patient experience and disease progression. Patients, or their caregivers or guardians, can enter information from anywhere in the world. The data is made anonymous and stored securely in an online portal called a registry. The XLH Network, Inc. may share the data but not your personal identifying information with individuals or institutions conducting research or clinical trials, as approved by the study's governing board that includes scientists, doctors and patient advocates.

The XLH Network, Inc. is launching the study in collaboration with the National Organization for Rare Disorders (NORD), an independent charity that built its natural history study platform as part of its mission to help identify and treat all 7,000 rare diseases. Funding is supported by a cooperative agreement between NORD and the U.S. Food and Drug Administration (FDA).

For more information, visit xlhnaturalhistory.iamrare.org. If you have questions, please contact registryinfo@xlhnetwork.org.

# OTHER RESOURCES

If you'd like to learn more about XLH (or the related phosphate-wasting disorders), here are some of our favorite resources:

**The XLH Network, Inc., social media**
Website: http://xlhnetwork.org/
Facebook: https://www.facebook.com/xlhnetwork/
Twitter: @XLH_Network
Forum: http://vps.xlhnetwork.org/~xlhforum/forum/

**Newsletter sign-up**
Contact ExecutiveDirector@XLHNetwork.org

**About the XLH Natural History Study**
https://xlhnaturalhistory.iamrare.org/

**Brochure for dental professionals**
http://xlhnetwork.org/files/9514/8441/9734/DentalProBrochure.pdf

**Find out about the latest clinical trials**
https://clinicaltrials.gov/

## Clinician's Guide to X-Linked Hypophosphatemia

*J Bone Miner Res*. 2011 Jul; 26(7): 1381–1388.

https://www.ncbi.nlm.nih.gov/pmc/articles/PMC3157040/

## National Organization for Rare Disorders (NORD)

https://rarediseases.org/rare-diseases/familial-hypophosphatemia/

## Other patient support groups:

French-speaking: http://www.rvrh.fr/

Peru: facebook.com/raqutismo.hipofosfatemicoperu

## Questions?

If you have more questions, you can contact us:

ExecutiveDirector@XLHNetwork.org

# CONTRIBUTORS

**Nancy J. Alauzen** is the oldest of six children and the only one in her family diagnosed with XLH. In her teens and twenties she believed that by surgically correcting the severe bowing would solve all of her XLH problems, not realizing that XLH had other complications. You can see pictures of Nancy at the first XLH Day at www.xlhnetwork.org/weak-bones-strong-wills.

**Anonymous** is a woman who inherited XLH from her mother and unfortunately passed it on to each of her sons.

**Helmut Barz** ticks like a clock (long story); he works as a professional storyteller and writer in Offenbach, Germany.

**Sheila Black** is the author of *House of Bone, Love/Iraq* (both CW Books), *Wen Kroy* (Dream Horse Press), and *Iron, Ardent* (Educe Press). She co-edited with Jennifer Bartlett and Michael Northen *Beauty is a Verb*: *The New Poetry of Disability*, (Cinco Puntos Press). In 2012 she received a Witter Bynner Fellowship from the Library of Congress. She lives in San Antonio, Texas where she directs Gemini Ink, a literary arts center.

**Lorna Brandt** is one of the older generation of spontaneous XLH cases, so was not afforded the early treatment that is now available, but through personal determination, as well as social and emotional support from family and friends, she has led as normal and successful a life as possible.

**Latrell Castanon** is a singer, Registered Nurse, and business owner born with XLH in Fort Worth, Texas. She was an adoptee as a baby and is now married with two kids and three grandsons, none of whom have XLH.

"**Kaggy**" is her nickname—unusual and unconventional, just like her adventurous and uplifting story about her strength of spirit in overcoming adversity as the only person in her birth family with spontaneous XLH.

**Valery Didula** is from Moscow, Russia, and is a guitarist who writes folk-rock music. You can see a picture of him in concert here: www.xlhnetwork.org/weak-bones-strong-wills or watch one of his concerts here:
 https://www.youtube.com/watch?v=_pRB-WrV6E8M.

**Geoff Edelson** was diagnosed with a spontaneous case of XLH as a child in 1962. He currently resides in Massachusetts with his wife and two children. Geoff is currently the Underwater Acoustics Technology Development Manager for BAE Systems Technology Solutions in Merrimack, New Hampshire.

**Jessica G**. is a mother, daughter, and athlete with XLH.

**Mary Hawley** has coped with XLH/VDRR by bicycling through life. She is on the extreme side of the disorder, reaching a natural height of only 4' 3" tall. Femur osteotomies enabled her to gain another four inches in height after her growth plates closed at twelve years old. Tenacity and determination come to mind to those that know her. You can see Mary Hawley and her trusty bicycle at www.xlhnetwork.org/weak-bones-strong-wills.

**Sheila G. Hunter** enjoys playing music, knitting, reading, writing, taking photos and building things out of wood, and yet still finds time to go to multiple medical appointments for her XLH.

**Joyce Olewski Inman** is an assistant professor of English at a university in the south, but she is first and foremost the mother of two lovely little girls—one of whom happens to have XLH.

**Marah Inman** is a seventh grader in south Mississippi. She enjoys photography, reading, and running.

**Sanders Inman** is a fourth grader in south Mississippi. She was diagnosed with XLH when she was two-and-a-half years old. She loves to read and do gymnastics. You can see her video about XLH as part of the National Organization for Rare Disorders' "Do Your Share" program here: http://doyourshare.com//?story=33.

**Gin Jones** is not a doctor, just a patient with a penchant for storytelling, quilting and reading medical journals.

**Rachael Jones** is married with two young children. She was a school administrator and now works in curriculum development as a textbook editor. Rachael enjoys writing and hopes to one day become a published children's book author. You can see her video about XLH as part of the National Organization for Rare Disorders' "Do Your Share" program here: http://doyourshare.com//?story=10.

**Michael Lamoureux** is a recent father and engineering graduate, born with XLH along with his twin brother. He strives to understand and reshape the boundaries of his abilities, with the goal of maintaining an active and healthy lifestyle. You can see a video about his experience with exercise as an XLHer here: https://vimeo.com/50954166.

**Kimberly Murray** is an XLH patient with a strong passion for living life to the fullest and enjoys watching her daughter Madelyn (also an XLH patient) develop the same positive attitude.

Some of **Elizabeth Olear**'s favorite people have XLH. She likes to read, travel, snuggle puppies, and cook for her family.

**Gini Patrick** is an aging XLHer who resides in a Southern Indiana college town where she spends most of her time on art, music, and writing.

**Raya Quereau** is a thoughtful and spunky nine-year-old who is diagnosed with XLH.

**Sarah Quereau** is an XLH patient and an XLH parent, who has learned many important lessons through her journey with XLH and has made it a goal to build her life around unconditional love and compassion.

**Jon Rann** has been an illustrator, commercial artist, musician, teacher, writer and toy collector. He has supported the use of computer technology for online teaching and learning within higher education for almost thirty years, and has supported a series of spoiled tomcats for even longer.

**Andrew Shortall** is an Irish-born XLHer who taught himself how to cook like a chef, enjoys wine and is a published short story writer with aspirations to become a novelist.

**Bess Thomason Smith** is a Christ follower, wife, caregiver, and elementary teacher who does not let XLH hinder her passion for all things creative.

**Marina Velazquez** has experience with XLH as a patient, daughter of an XLH patient, and mother of two gorgeous daughters affected with XLH.

**Chris Younger** is a spontaneous XLHer who works very hard to keep on keeping on with a disease that keeps on giving.

**Rustam Zinnatullin** is from the Republic of Bashkortostan in Russia. He has XLH and is a champion weight-lifter. You can see a picture of Rustam at www.xlhnetwork.org/weak-bones-strong-wills

**Bryan from Missouri** is an adult with XLH, currently pursuing a graduate degree in computer science, who overall considers any past and present medical issues to have made life rather interesting. In his spare time he enjoys dancing, videography, reading, baking, acting, sports, and theoretical physics, as time allows, of course.

**Carol from Missouri** is an adult XLH patient from Missouri who *still* likes to know everything she can! She even does online research before traveling so she can know which unique buildings or menu items to look for when she arrives.

80195363R00093

Made in the USA
Columbia, SC
06 November 2017